Blasco de Grañén

THE MATTHIESEN GALLERY
7/8, Mason's Yard, Duke Street St. James's,
London, SW1Y 6BU

Matthiesen Ltd.

7/8, Mason's Yard, Duke Street St. James's,
London, SW1Y 6BU
Tel: (+44) 20 7930 2437 Fax: (+44) 20 7930 1387

E-mail: Gallery@MatthiesenGallery.com
Web: www.MatthiesenGallery.com

In association with

COLL&CORTÉS

Justiniano, 3 28004 Madrid, Spain
Tel: +34 91 310 05 82 Fax: +34 91 310 06 48
e-mail: info@collcortes.com

THIS CATALOGUE
IS DEDICATED TO THE MEMORY
OF THOSE PRECURSORS OF 'THE MONUMENTS MEN'
WHO RISKED LIFE AND LIMB 1936-1939 TO SALVAGE ART
FROM THE MAELSTROM OF THE SPANISH CIVIL WAR

Preface

his is the second of a duo of publications that we are issuing in 2015 dedicated to Spanish Art. It is a companion to that on Juan de Sevilla. Both publications discuss aspects of early or mid-fifteenth century Castilian and Aragonese art. The present volume addresses the iconography and workshop practice of Blasco de Grañén and his associates.

Once again I am very grateful to Judith Sobre for finding the time to write on Blasco during her busy teaching schedule. I also record my thanks to Nuria Ortiz Valero for her essay on the Crucifixion and its iconography. Judith, in the course of discussions, mentioned the existence of little known passages in José Gudiol Ricart's *Memoirs* relating to his activity, early on during the Spanish Civil War, saving art from the mindless and destructive forces then in play. Together, we thought that it would be both relevant and of interest to our readers if we included these here and Judith was gracious enough not only to translate the passages from Catalan and Spanish, the first time that they appear in print in English, but also to write a short introduction. As Blasco and several of his works are referred to in this piece, I have incorporated this text as the Introduction to this catalogue and as a prelude to the discussion of Blasco's *Crucifixion* which is then analysed in greater detail. Some of the photos in the text are of poor quality as they date from 1936 or earlier and the paintings were damaged or destroyed. At a distance of almost eighty years one can only be both astonished and horrified by the cataclysm that descended upon Spain as Fascism spread across Europe just before World War Two.

I thank Damaso Berenguer for acting as our 'point man' in Spain and Elisa Foster for arranging a translation of Nuria Ortiz Valero's text. I express gratitude to José Antonio Tolosa; to Julie Burgess Conklin of the Grand Rapids Art Museum; to Daniel Perez; to the Special Collections, Fine Arts Library, Harvard University; to the Museo Ibercaja Camón Aznar, all for assisting us with images; to Studio Ticci for another delicate conservation treatment; to Prudence Cuming Associates for photography. I must particularly mention the indispensable Clare Wadsworth for her falcon-like eye as the back-up proof reader; to Sara Hobday but above all to Judith Sobre who demonstrated reserves of patience which are quite unusual as we struggled to edit and repeatedly refine texts and obtain elusive images thus resulting in a dozen proofs.

PATRICK MATTHIESEN

Introduction to Gudiol's account of the Spanish Civil War

osep Gudiol i Ricart's role as a Catalan 'Monuments Man' during the Spanish Civil war (1936-1939) was not at all unique. In the turbulent days and months following General Francisco Franco's coup d'état of July 18, 1936, that triggered the war, a large number of volunteers were actively engaged in rescuing artworks from destruction, and not uniquely in Catalonia.[1] Unlike the work of the American, French and British 'Monuments Men' at the end of World War II, involving the hunting down of European works of art looted by the Nazis, those in Spain were working during a civil conflict that involved constantly shifting boundaries and numerous factions. In the case of the Republic, and particularly in Catalonia, then far from the front, there was at times a civil war within the civil war with various groups of Anarcho-Syndicalists, Socialists, Marxists, some allied with Stalin and others independent, Catalan Nationalists of both left and centre and other fringe groups battling for supremacy.

For anyone not right there and participating, the series of acronyms used by these various groups was and still is dizzying. George Orwell, who fought as a volunteer with a non-Stalinist Marxist group, the P.U.O.M. (Partit Obrer d'Unificació Marxista), talks about his initial confusion with the numerous factions in his book *Homage to Catalonia*:

> 'As for the kaleidoscope of political parties and trade unions, with their tiresome names - P.S.U.C., P.O.U.M., F.A.I., C.N.T., U.G.T., J.C.I., J.S.U., A.I.T - they merely exasperated me. It looked at first sight as though Spain were suffering from a plague of initials. I knew that I was serving in something called the P.O.U.M. (I had only joined the P.O.U.M. militia rather than any other because I happened to arrive in Barcelona with I.L.P. [Independent Labour Party papers], but I did not realize that there were serious differences between the political parties.'[2]

---

1. For an account of the big picture of Catalan art rescuers at this time, see, Francisco Gracia and Gloria Munilla, *Salvem l'art: la protecció del patrimony cultural català durant la guerra civil,* Barcelona, La Magrana, 2011. A briefer English summary of these events can be found in Miriam M Basilio, *Visual Propaganda, Exhibitions, and the Spanish Civil War*, Farnham, Ashgate Publishing Limited, 2013, pp.86-93.

In Barcelona rumours of an impending coup had been circulating for some weeks before the event and plans were being made to repulse Fascist troops stationed on the west side of the city in barracks near Pedralbes when the signal for Franco's landing came. These troops were under the command of General Manuel Goded Lopis, who was to arrive by seaplane from Mallorca. The Fascist revolt began in the city before dawn on the 18th. By the time General Goded arrived, at 1 p.m., the Fascists had been defeated by the combined efforts of numerous militia companies raised by various Anarchist, Trade Union, Marxist, Socialist and Catalanista groups, along with assault troops and municipal police - the *Mossos d'Escuadra* ('Guys of the Squadron') who remained loyal to the Republic. Goded was promptly imprisoned, and executed a few days later.

Euphoria quickly got out of hand, as it did elsewhere where the initial coup was repulsed. Spontaneous riots broke out and the main targets were those considered reactionary elements: the church, rural landowners and, in Catalonia, the rich bourgeoisie and industrialists.[3] Uncontrolled gangs not only of individual militia groups, but also opportunistic individuals and convicted criminals, who were sprung from municipal jails on July 19th, rampaged through Barcelona and other Catalan cities, as well as smaller towns and villages throughout the region. The most conspicuous targets were churches, for the Church had long been long viewed as one of the linchpins of Spanish wealth and conservatism and, by extension, in cahoots with the oppressive rich. Churches were burned, often along with their furniture and perishable altarpieces, both mediæval and more recent, and objects made of precious materials were taken. Often the attacking gangs opened tombs, dumping out the human remains and robbing those as well. Sometimes the perpetrators were local, but just as often the raiders came from the outside, destroying one village church after another and sometimes liquidating those whom they considered right-wingers as well.[4]

In Barcelona, the mansions of rich industrialists, long despised by their underpaid workers, were attacked and looted. There seemed to be no definite or systematic preplanned destruction, rather a series of undisciplined

---

2. George Orwell, *Homage to Catalonia* Boston, Beacon Press, 1955, p.47
    Orwell fought on the Aragonese Front with the P.S.U.C. in 1936-1937. His is the clearest account in English of what was happening in Catalonia and Aragon during the period Dec. 1936 – July 1937.
3. Targets varied, conservatives in other regions included aristocrats, Monarchists and Carlists among others.
4. An excellent account of the chaotic days of the nearly-complete disorder in Barcelona and other Catalan towns and cities can be found in Paul Preston, *The Spanish Holocaust: Inquisition and Extermination in Twentieth-Century Spain,* New York, W.W. Norton & Company, 2013, Chapter pp.221-258

assaults that broke out simultaneously, certainly reinforced by the fact that one of the largest factions were, the Anarchists (F.A.I.). Sometimes the attacks were ideological, at other times seemingly at random. The F.A.I. newspaper, Solidaridad Obrera, gives one such account of the sacking of the house of Joan Pich i Pon, a favourite and scandalous industrialist and politician:

> 'The People have invaded the residence of the plutocrat Don Pich y Pon.
> Yesterday morning, the people penetrated the sumptuous mansion that the regrettably celebrated Don Juan Pich y Pon owns on the Plaza de Cataluña.
> The workers have taken out the furnishings. They have trampled, with the classic grandeur of public anger, upon objects of very high value with which he had exalted himself and which he had accumulated in his lair from the chests of the abundance of the Barcelona municipality.'[5]

osep Gudiol i Ricart, 31 years old in 1936, became a participant, along with others, not in the destruction of objects, but rather in saving them from the looters attacking churches and wealthy residences in the name of Catalonia's artistic patrimony. Five years later, he wrote an account of his rescuing activities during the Civil War in Catalonia and Aragon. The reason for his writing it at that time had to do with the process of 'purification' which would enable him to return to Franco's Spain in that year and to demonstrate that he had not been a 'red.'[6] The account has been published twice, once as part of a collection entitled *Tres Escritos de Josep María Gudiol i Ricart*, just after his death.[7] More recently, it was published online as part of the doctoral dissertation of Guillem Cañameras Vall (2013), *La trajectória de Josep Gudiol Ricart entre 1930 i 1940: Contribucions i aportacions al seu estudi.*, with additional material edited out of the printed version and some of the published passages omitted.[8]

---

5.   *Solaridad Obrera,* Barcelona, 24th July, 1936, p. 4
6.   The Franco Regime generally designated all left-leaning organizations as "reds."
7.   Josep Maria Gudiol i Ricart, *Tres Escritos de Josep María Gudiol i Ricart*, Barcelona Minora, 1987.
8.   *diposit.ub.edu/dspace/bitstream/…/Gudiol_Ricart.pdf.* Esborrany de «En su defensa: la intervención de Josep Gudiol en el Salvamento del Patrimonio Artístico durante la Guerra Civil»,

osep Gudiol, born into a comfortably middle-class family, had grown up within the still developing field of art history. His uncle, Josep Gudiol i Cunill, was both a cleric and an expert in Catalan antiquities and mediæval culture and director of the Archeological Museum in Vic, who had received part of his training in Italy. The younger Josep had his formal training in architecture and in 1936 he was Architect for the Museu d'Arqueología in Barcelona, a position that was less grand than it sounds. However, Gudiol's real enthusiasm was for art history and his attractive personality, intelligence and demeanour were helpful in his continuing education and in making contacts with wealthy art patrons in Barcelona. All of this was to contribute to his profound knowledge of the visual arts of Catalonia that was to serve him throughout his life. Most importantly for his future, his art historian uncle introduced him to Doña Teresa Amatller, the unmarried sole heiress to a prosperous chocolate factory, who lived in an opulent *modernista* house on the smartest street in town, the Passeig de Gràcia. Senyora Amatller had earlier adopted a child who died young and she eventually regarded Gudiol as the son she never had.[9] She also had a formidable art collection.

By the age of 25, he had been taken under the wing of Professor Walter W.S. Cook, director of the Institute of Fine Arts in New York (New York University's graduate department of Art History). Cook brought him to the United States in 1930-31 to further his education.

When Franco invaded, Gudiol had been traveling in the South of France with Dr. Cook and his colleague from Harvard, Chandler Post, and they had just arrived back in Barcelona. With turbulent conditions in the city, both Americans left Spain as soon as they could. Meanwhile, Gudiol had spent the weekend with his wife and daughters out in a suburban town with other family members.

When news of the burning of churches and the looting of houses reached him, Gudiol's decision to return to Barcelona and try to rescue artworks put him in some peril. Some radical groups regarded art as an extension of the church and wished to destroy it; others respected it and turned much of it in to the Catalan government, the Generalitat, for safekeeping. Rescuers were sometimes mistaken for looters and shot (a fate that Gudiol nearly suffered later in Aragon).

---

9.   This anecdotal biographical material was conveyed in various conversations the author had with Dr. Joan Ainaud de Lasarte in 1975-76.

Most of the artists and art historians who participated in rescue efforts regarded artworks, especially mediæval ones, as part of Catalonia's artistic patrimony, harking back to the 'Golden Age' of Catalan hegemony during the 13th through the 15th centuries. This gave them the status of cultural relics, apart from their religious functions. In this they reflected the point of view of the Catalan Republican government, which took pains to get this message out to the public, forty per cent of whom were illiterate. To reinforce this point of view among the working class Union and Anarchist members, they also tried to make the point that these objects were the product of honest labour.[10] In 1937 the most radical group, the Anarcho-Syndicalists of the F.A.I - C.N.T, would stage their own exhibition of objects they had rescued. The Museu d'Art and the Museu d'Arqueológica of Barcelona became the repositories for rescued artworks and the Museum administrations were quick to take credit for the rescue operations.[11]

Gudiol participated in these operations both in and out of Barcelona and it was his organisational skills that were most useful: collecting data and making lists of what was brought in, whatever group did the rescuing, and trying to help systematize the gathering of objects in a logical way, rather than the random rescue of objects by random people during the first few days.

He also went out to outlying towns and villages and, when he could, prevented the total burning down of churches by persuading the attackers to use the space as a concert hall or other public functional space. During this period many churches served as garages, stables and warehouses.

In neighbouring Aragon things were much dicier. Gudiol records the sculptor Apel.les Fenosa bringing back the surviving parts of the *Retablo Mayor* of Lanaja (we have already seen Fenosa's account of this rescue from the other side). But in Aragon, where the illiteracy rate was higher, the war was raging. Many of the front line Republican soldiers were F.A.I Anarchists and there was also much more destruction.[12] Gudiol mentions his own experiences at Sijena and his near-death in Alquezar. It is Fenosa who best captures the state of mind of the Aragonese who regarded the Catalans as arrogant colonisers:

---

10. Basilio, p. 88.
11. 'la revolució de Juliol i els nostres museus d'art,' *Butlletí dels museus d'art de Barcelona*, no. 65, 1936, pp. 301 – 318. This article also gave the chain of command in these activities, many of whom are mentioned by Gudiol in his account.
12. But there was also a far greater degree of rough-hewn equality. See Orwell, p. 27.

'I arrived at midday in Pallaruegro de Monegros with an ambulance, while there were so many people that passed by in cars, showing off, we were saving millions and millions and there was no way to find a touring car. I found a formidable *retablo* ten meters high, disassembled in the patio of the Committee. They wanted to chop it up for firewood for the winter! After arguing with everyone who thought I was a Fascist, I was able to put three pieces inside the church. The Committee promised me that they would shelter the rest while I looked for means of transport. I was afraid that it would rain. I went around as fast as possible but a heavy downpour almost destroyed the *retablo*. The committee, to whom I had promised a teacher and a library, wouldn't let me take the drenched *retablo* because they wanted a truck in payment. 'But if this has no value for you leave it to get soaked and be destroyed' I told them. 'For us, no' they replied, ' but it has value as firewood; we see that for you it's worth a lot, so pay it!' And, since I didn't have a truck to give them, the *retablo* remained there. How much money did it represent? It was a jewel and, under the rain and the sun, nothing will remain.'[13]

On the other hand, Orwell's account of serving in Aragon at that time makes the citizens of Pallaruego de Monegros' point of view understandable. It was bitterly cold, there were no trees, little available firewood and for ordinary people, any wood, even with paint on it, was a necessity to avoid freezing to death.[14]

As was the case with many industrialists whose houses were invaded and sacked, Teresa Amatller's collection was in peril. Gudiol prevented its being looted and when Amatller left the country she put him in charge of her house. He made good use of it, setting up a workshop there to repair damaged works of art. He also helped Amatller financially during the war years, sending her money when he could and also getting Cook to send her funds from the United States.

In 1937, Gudiol was called up into the army and managed, with his degree in architecture, to become a fortifications engineer. He continued his rescue operations whenever he could, until Franco's victory in 1939 forced him over the border into France. His friend Dr. Cook managed to get him a job photographing Romanesque monuments in France but, with the Nazi invasion, he went to the United States. His family remained in Barcelona and for the next two years, while teaching and curating exhibitions in America, he worked on plans to get home.

---

13. *Mirador. Setmanari de Literatura, Art i Politica*, Any VIII Núm 397, Barcelona, dijous, 3 desembre 1936 (segona epoca), pp.8
14. Orwell, p.30

Having served in the Spanish Republican army, Gudiol was definitely *persona non grata* during the initial years of the Franco regime but Teresa Amatller, now back in Barcelona with her impeccable bourgeois credentials, worked to bring him back. He was finally able to return in 1941 but not without going through 'purification.' In order to do this, he was obliged to plead his case and his narrative stems from that process.

He was eventually cleared, yet was forbidden to practice architecture or hold any government position. Amatller again came to his rescue, establishing the Institut Amatller d'Art Històric in her mansion and she put Gudiol in charge of it. He remained in that position for the next 40 years.

Gudiol's account of his activities during the Civil War is very vivid, particularly in evoking the first frenzied weeks of the 1936 revolt when he was truly working 'on the ground' as an eyewitness as well as a rescuer. It is difficult to know what he auto-censored and what really happened due to his necessity to satisfy the Franco government. When I got to know him in the mid-1960s, he and most of the Catalans who had been active on the Republican side and were then working in Barcelona were treading a fine line between their lip service to the regime and what they really thought.

It was only after Franco's death in 1975 that things could be viewed from a more honest perspective. A real appreciation of Gudiol had to wait even longer in fact, until a symposium commemorating the 25th anniversary of his death in 2012 was held, appropriately at the Institut Amatller, and Guillem Cañameras Vall's dissertation in 2013. Both the event presentations and the dissertation are, appropriately enough, in Catalan. It is time that a wider public be made aware of his activities.

JUDITH SOBRE

Memoirs of a Monuments Man[1]

eturning from an excursion to the South of France, I arrived in Barcelona on the night of July 17, 1936, with Professor Chandler R. Post of Harvard University. The next morning we visited the Museu d'Art de Catalunya along with Dr. Walter S. Cook, Director of the Institute of Fine Arts. We had planned a very interesting investigative archaeological journey through the north of Spain for months and decided to set off the following Monday, July 20. I left them at the Hotel Colón and went to Torrellas de Llobregat to spend the weekend with my family. Torellas is a little town 20 kms from Barcelona.

The first rumours were broadcast on the radio with surprising and contradictory proclamations. Battles, fires and crimes were mentioned, but nothing definite. The commentaries, broadcast from town to town, claimed that not even the greatest historic and artistic jewels had escaped the flames and that the famous churches of Belén, El Pino and Santa María del Mar, Santa Ana as well as many other marvels of old Barcelona were burning. They said that the same thing was happening to churches all over our country. We went up to the top of a nearby hill from which we could see the city of Barcelona and, in effect, black columns of smoke confirmed the dramatic news. Returning from this vivid spectacle, we found the church in the little town of Torrellas on fire. A group of armed men had also set fire to the parish house and to benches piled up in the centre of the church. They had arrived in a truck, firing their hunting rifles, and left immediately after setting the fire. The people of Torellas threw themselves into extinguishing it and luckily the damage was minor. So we stayed on a day longer, waiting for news, out of touch with everyone, listening with friends and neighbours to the proclamations, decrees and news items broadcast from Barcelona and Seville. Our nerves could not stand it a moment longer. Contrary to the

---

1. These diary notes were made by Gudiol Ricart and are published here for the first time in English. They were originally transcribed at a conference in Bareclona in 1987 and have partially appeared in: *diposit.ub.edu/dspace/bitstream/…/Gudiol_ Ricart.pdf.* Esborrany de «En su defensa: la intervención de Josep Gudiol en el Salvamento del Patrimonio Artístico durante la Guerra Civil»; and Gudiol Ricart, Josep. *Tres escritos de Josep Maria Gudiol i Ricart.* Barcelona: Arturo Ramón i Manuel Barbié, 1987. [transcribed from the conference notes]

1936 The Sack of Santa Maria del Mar.

advice of our families a group of friends decided to go on foot to Barcelona. We left at four in the morning on July 22. Having passed through Sant Boi de Llobregat and Cornellá we soon found barricades and evidence of struggles. Groups of armed men controlled the entrance and exit to every town. The road to Barcelona was a real problem because the infamous safe-conducts were already in circulation, full of seals and improvised stamps. Finally, at eleven that morning, we arrived at Barcelona's Plaza de España.

I immediately went to Santa Maria del Mar. Through its broken doors, the black and still blisteringly hot vaulting of this marvellous church showed pilasters chipped by fire. Outside mountains of burned paper, twisted ironwork, broken stained glass and fragments of gilded *retablos* filled streets and sidewalks. I began to pick up the fragments of a well-known Gothic stained glass window and was detained by armed men who, fortunately, took me for an inquisitive foreigner and freed me after a few minutes.

It seemed like a surreal nightmare to see a monument that I believed to be one of the jewels of everyone's soul destroyed. Continuing my dramatic pilgrimage, I walked towards the Church of Santa María del Pi, crossing the Plaça de Sant Jaume. The *Generalitat* was an anthill. Tieless functionaries and militiamen with four-day beards pushed each other at the entrance and overflowed at the windows. By chance I bumped into my friend Gibert, an official of the Barcelona Museum. He asked me to come with him to the office of Ventura

Gassol, Councillor of Culture of the *Generalitat* because something had to be done to avoid more destruction. We made our way through the surging mob and horrible though picturesque crowds filling patios, passages and buildings. Gassol's office heaved with people. A group of men were smashing some precious metalwork they had found in a strongbox in the sacristy of Santa María del Pi and which they had opened with a blowtorch. These were the reliquaries and monstrances of the Church of Sant Just, as well as mountains of valuables and even packets of banknotes. Joaquím Folch i Torres Bosch Gimpera, the president of the *Círcol Artìstic* and other people well known in art circles were there, commenting on the terrible events. They spoke of the most inconceivable destruction: they thought the Vic Museum had been burned, the Cathedral of Manresa with its entire collection of primitives, the Museum of Solsona. They did not know anything definite about Lleida or Girona, Tarragona, Seu d'Urgell, etc. They showed me the *retablos* from the Diocesan Museum of Barcelona piled up on a ground floor, saved from the flames and the sacking of the seminary by a group of artists led by the sculptor Otero, who, with some trucks borrowed by Melchior Font, Gassol's secretary, had rescued a substantial part of the contents from the flames. Some objects clearly showed the effects of fire; others perished when a truck was set on fire in the street by an unidentified group who viewed it as a transport of 'saints.' They told me that the Cathedral was intact and guarded by the police and that they had saved the churches of Sant Just, Sant Sever and Santa Clara from being set on fire because they were near the *Ajuntament* and *Generalitat*. The Catalan police were guarding the Convent of Pedralbes, also intact so far. There was no trouble at the Museums of Art and Archeology or at the *Archivo de la Corona de Aragón*.

group of volunteers and museum employees reinforced the doors of churches and houses containing things of artistic value in neighbouring towns; large posters proclaimed that the building and contents of the *Generalitat de Catalunya* had been seized.

Folch i Torres, Director of the Art Museum, and Bosch i Gimpera, Director of the Archeological Museum, began feverishly organizing the work, making arrangements to prevent more losses and safeguard endangered objects. I, who was only the Archeological Museum architect, offered my services and asked if they could put me in the group which, driven solely by its love of art, had gathered at the Culture Council office. We began work immediately. Together with Gibert, who was working intensively, we went to the burned churches. Our first visit was to Santa Ana, which was still smoking. We were able to recover two gothic Virgins intact, but the magnificent gothic panels of Serra and Bermejo had perished in the fire. The stone lacework of the rose window in Santa Maria del Pi was smashed and no longer in situ; the altars were almost entirely spared by the fire, which had completely destroyed the baroque Chapel of the Holy Blood and calcinated the precious sculptures on the bosses of the vaulting. The admirable Gothic Virgin that presided over the main doorway was in her place, but blackened by smoke. The interior of the Church of Belén had completely perished, together with its baroque *retablos,* paintings by Viladomat, marbles and stuccowork. Its magnificent stone facades still stood, hiding the terrible emptiness of its interior.

Exhausted, both mentally and spiritually, by this drama and the long pilgrimage of July 22, I went to Passeig de Gràcia 41 the next day, the 23rd, the home of Mme. Teresa Amatller, who had one of the best art collections in Barcelona. One of the first columns of voluntary militia was lined up in front. Luckily we arrived in time to save the private collections. The churches, as we learned when contact was established with the towns, had suffered enormously after a general order to burn them. Those that were not burned had their contents completely destroyed, whether of artistic value or not. Sometimes though, an inexplicable miracle of conservation occurred.

The next morning I went directly to the *Generalitat.* Furniture, books and papers were violently flying out of the windows of one of the houses on the Plaça de Sant Jaume. They were sacking the apartment of Milá i Camps. I recovered a 15th century manuscript from the books falling into the gutter. It was a treatise on horses with magnificent drawings. I gave it to Mr. Jordi Rubió. Other houses were also being violently ransacked and a store selling religious objects was emptied in a few minutes: thousands of little prints covered the plaza, together with furniture, clothing and books. I went up to Gassol's office and he, with tears in his eyes, telephoned the Government Councillor to avoid the terrible searches called 'registrations' that, after this sinister beginning, quickly spread throughout Barcelona right in front of the helpless authorities like a powdering of dust. Mestres, Minister of Government, answered that he had no forces at his disposal and that it was impossible to avoid the madness that always ended with the burning of smashed furniture in front of the sacked house. Thus began the looting and 'registering', a euphemism for robbery.

In some cases, the protective posters nailed up the day before didn't prevent either the sacking or 'registering.' The 'registering' groups carried part of their booty to the *Generalitat* and departments were filled with boxes of deeds, stocks and bonds, statues, paintings, silver objects, radios, typewriters, etc. Folch put me to work classifying groups of more or less artistic elements and, with a group of volunteers, I began to take inventory and pack up pieces to be sent to the Museum. Silver objects of artistic or archaeological value were given to a special commission. This work was carried out in the Librarian's School. In this way I began to set up a rudimentary group to save our artistic patrimony. However, something more was required: it was necessary to act very rapidly because unforeseen disorganization and overriding anarchy pervaded everything. Groups of artists went out to save artistic patrimony on their own and elements from the burned churches and private collections were rapidly assembled. Immediately diverse groups of rescuers began spontaneously to battle with the group from the *Generalitat*. In the middle of rescuing the gothic panels from the Retailer's Guild a disgraceful discussion broke out in the middle of the Plaça del Pi between the artists who had seized the paintings and delegates of the *Generalitat*. Some of these struggles were reported in *Solidaridad Obrera,* accusing a *Generalitat* group of protecting private interests.[2] My first job was to coordinate all of these impulsive, sometimes counterproductive, art rescue groups and try to centralize all of them at the *Generalitat*.

This was a crazy and very difficult task. There was no law, order or authority and it was difficult to obtain trucks and gasoline for the groups. We did not have any control over the situation, but continued hopefully, without being able to confirm anything from most of the other districts of Catalonia.

---

2. The rhetoric of the moment can be seen in an article from *Solaridad Obrera, Barcelona*, 24th July, 1936, p. 4:
   'THE PEOPLE HAVE INVADED THE RESIDENCE OF THE PLUTOCRAT DON PICH Y PON.
   Yesterday morning, the people penetrated the sumptuous mansion that the regrettably celebrated Don Juan Pich y Pon owns on the Plaza de Cataluña.
   The workers have removed the furnishings and have trampled with the classic grandeur of public anger upon these objects of very high value with which he had exalted himself and which were accumulated in his lair.
   Popular nemesis has descended upon Pich y Pon. In the acts carried out by the people yesterday, he has paid for the immorality and insolence of a politician who enriches himself at the expense of the public. A bit of sanitation has been performed. This is the conduct that the working class must pursue against all the bandits and holdup men, dandies in brocade.'

he disorder increased and the 'registering' groups got bigger. By this time, the posters put up by the *Generalitat* to respect property were being totally ignored. Hoping for results, many people in Barcelona got copies of this poster and put it on their doors even though they had not even one object of artistic interest. This resulted in the total disaccreditation of the posters, which became a real danger and incited 'registers.' The only secure refuges were the municipal museums and the only solution was to seize artworks. Orders of seizure included the Amatller, Rocamora, Marsana, Macaya, Cambó, Guell, Muntadas and other collections, just to protect them.

The first four were offered by their owners or authorized representatives. Other less important collectors, not included in the decrees, went to the *Generalitat* and asked me to include them. Among these I remember the Capmany, Martí, Simó, Vallín, Vilella Collections and many others which had only one painting or a little artistic nucleus that they voluntarily offered the museum. There followed an avalanche of petitions offering paintings and sculpture that in the majority of cases were objects of little interest, insistently offered up in fear of the terrible religious persecution and iconoclastic mania unfolding in Catalunya.

In other cases, collections were not seized because the proprietors or their authorized representatives assured us that they could guarantee their integrity. This was the case with the Mateu family, whose representative was Mr. Clausells. He was assassinated a few weeks after the revolution exploded. Their collections were in a warehouse on the *Calle de los Ángeles*, in the home of L. Miguel Mateu on the *Paseo de Gràcia* and in that of D. Damian Mateu on the *Diagonal*. One day we received casual notice that the latter two had been sacked. I went myself to both apartments and was still able to rescue a large number of paintings, the majority of them smashed, as well as some of the cameos from the famous Mateu Collection. The pieces kept at the warehouse on the *Carrer dels Angels* suffered no damage at all and were willingly handed over to the *Generalitat* by the committee that directed the society. The collection of the Widow Bosch was not taken in the belief that it had already been burned. I think it was the house servants who informed us that a railway workers' committee had installed itself in the apartment, smashing doors, looking for hidden treasures and carrying away objects. The sculptor Durán, one of most active of the group of artistic retrievers, presented himself at the door of the Bosch house and was received by a man holding a pistol. Only after lengthy altercation was he able to rescue some of the collection. It goes without saying that all the gold and silver objects had disappeared. Mr. Soler i March, the architect, who had some gothic *retablos* of great importance, begged us not to take them to the museum since he had a secure way to protect them. After a few months he came to the *Generalitat* requesting us to look for these *retablos,* which had been stolen from the French Chapel where he had kept them.

Another lamentable case, the worst of all, was that of the collection of Mr. Cambó, whose house had been occupied from the beginning by the F.A.I. Thanks to the laborious and able negotiations of Mr. Gibert, some of the famous paintings from the collection were handed over to the museum. Unfortunately, however, others were shot full of holes, ripped or cut.

I oversaw this seizure of collections. First thing in the morning I would give a list of the contents of the collection to be dealt with to the volunteers gathered at the Canons' House, and continue to sort through the many reports and notices arriving from all directions. I worked many hours classifying the objects brought to the *Generalitat*, which, carefully packed, were then transported to the museum. There they were handed over along with a receipt for the inventory. From the beginning, Mr. Pujol acted as general secretary of this improvised service collecting art and he continued in this role throughout the entire war.

The packing and inventory of each collection was carried out by specialized personnel from the museum, directed by volunteers. The Amatller Collection was inventoried and supervised by Robert i Llompart, who knew it well. The same group listed and packed up the Macaya Collection with the aid of some of the Macaya family. Marco and Sarsanedas inventoried and put together the enormous Masana Collection. Bardolet, among others, directed the packing of the Güell Collection, Colominas, that of García Faria, etc.

I suppose that the Monuments Section of Barcelona still [in 1941] preserves copies of the many written communications, orders and receipts that were issued and that show the quantity of work done in just a few days. With no expectation of remuneration all this work was carried out by the group of volunteers. On the initiative of Folch and Bosch, I was in charge from the very first moment. I had no official title and only an authorization signed by Gassol to be able to circulate freely. This was my contribution to the protection of our artistic patrimony and the various municipal and military governments who helped me can corroborate it.

fter a few days Mr. Jerónimo Martorell, Chief Architect of the Monuments Section, presented himself to the *Generalitat* and took over the direction of this work. On the afternoon of the 24th I was able to get the group of soldiers, who had brought the treasure of the church of El Pi to the *Generalitat*, to take me to Vic in a car that they had requisitioned. The trip was an ordeal of detentions and explanations at the entrance and exit points of each town, but despite these obstacles and many wrecked cars on the highway we arrived in Vic. The vaulting of the Cathedral continued to burn slowly and the lower windows of the Episcopal Palace, whose second floor housed the museum, belched thick smoke. I went to the *Ajuntament* and spoke with the Mayor, who told me that he had no authority and that I should make an agreement with the Revolutionary Committee. The latter was meeting, but after a long wait they received me. I showed the President the document signed by Gassol certifying my mission. They told me that for them it held no value since neither the Central Committee nor the Militias had issued it. They promised that they would protect the museum if it were truly a purely cultural institution and that they would authorize the firemen to put out the fire still burning on the ground floor of the Episcopal Palace.

In the Cathedral the fire had spared the High Altar and most of the other altars. The archive was the only place where the doors remained closed. The sacristy and the treasury were full of ecclesiastical garments and broken furniture. Most of Sert's paintings had been burned but the compositions of the *Capilla Mayor* remained intact and so did most of the interior of the façade. The silver sarcophagus of Sant Bernard Calvó was on the ground floor, but was relatively well preserved. In the Cathedral Plaza children played with vestments. On my return to Barcelona I begged Gassol to send forces to protect what remained of the Cathedral and he asked the militias to send reserves to guard the site.

On the afternoon of the next day, the *Generalitat* gave me a car driven by a policeman and, after obtaining a document with all the necessary seals, I returned to Vic. There the militiamen sent by Gassol to protect the Cathedral continued to ransack it, opening tombs and smashing everything. Having found the valuables of the ecclesiastic collection of the Vic Bishopric, the militiamen were inspired to look for more money and they did not respect anything. The Committee resented a troop of militia having been sent without first consulting them and proposed that, given the artistic value of the museum, a guard of people they trusted be formed. Josep Mialet, the janitor of the Vic Society of Tourism, was elected Chief of the Museum Guards. I promised them that I would take care of the payments to the six museum guards and Mialet at 10 pesetas a day. I used the reduced store of cash of which, as treasurer of the Vic Museum, I had custody. Later, these guards were paid by the *Generalitat*, since they were consigned by them to Vic. The Cathedral, Episcopal Palace and the museum were all closed. Mialet acquitted himself well and thwarted the Committee's idea of seizing those museum objects thought too religious, so that only the furniture was lost.

Until the day of my mobilization I continued to make at least a weekly visit to the Museum of Vic. On one visit a committee, at the insistence of Mialet, was showing the treasures of the Cathedral scattered over the floor of the meeting room of the *Ajuntament*, preparatory to melting them down. I insisted that they hand over to me at least the pieces of greatest artistic value. It was useless: everything was melted down and the *Generalitat* could do nothing about it. The committees were the absolute rulers of lives and fortunes and everyone remembers vividly how they used this infinite power. I could never find out who saved the big 14th century silver crucifix that turned up at the museum two years later.

eanwhile the Barcelona group continued working without respite. Folch i Torres took over control of the Cathedral, the Convent of Santa Clara and other religious buildings around the *Generalitat*. These were guarded by the police, whose first action was to steal all the collection boxes from the altars. This money allowed them to establish a reserve at the San Ivo portal of the Cathedral and keep going. The technical personnel of the museum dismantled the big gothic *retablos* and the baroque structures in the Cathedral and Santa Clara and Sant Felip and they were taken to the museum. The unions also insisted that the modern *retablos* be burned on Montjuïc by the fire brigade. But Folch was quickly obliged to hide this when The *Soledad Obrera* group began a campaign against keeping him on as director of the museum.

Finally the Commission for the Artistic, Historic and Scientific Patrimony of the *Generalitat* met and agreed to divide the rescuers into three groups, each one under an autonomous director with full powers to resolve matters himself. The archives remained under Agostí Durán, the libraries under Jordi Rubió and the monuments and material patrimony under Jeróni Martorell. I was given the job of coordinating all the work being done throughout Catalonia under Martorell. Identity cards were printed for everyone in these Departments of Protection of the Patrimony.

I immediately tried to organize links with other cities. Documents and objets d'art came to us from everywhere.

One of the first deliveries was from Seu d'Urgell. Mr. Canturri, with the aid of some assault guards, was able to prevent the burning of the Cathedral, although its furniture was destroyed and its canonical dependencies sacked. Canturri hid the archive in a secure place and brought part of the Cathedral's gems to Barcelona, including the Cross a 16th century reliquary and the famous 11th century *Beatus* manuscript. Unfortunately, the 15th century chalice and the richly illuminated 14th century missal had disappeared, as well as most of the Cathedral's manuscripts. Some town committees came to offer objects they thought to be of artistic interest saved from the sack of the Cathedral. It was therefore necessary to visit each small town, establish contacts, appoint committees and then immediately make an inventory of objects already saved to avoid their future destruction.

The unplanned groups in different towns were legalized quickly as and when contact with them was made. In Gerona, the Cathedral and museums remained under a delegation whose most active member was Mr. Tobias [Sobias?]. In Tarragona the artists Mallol and Rebull were chosen to guard the Cathedral and the museums and to inventory and protect the region. I sent a car over that had been voluntarily donated by its owner, L. Bosch. In Manresa, Mr. Rubiralta, aided by fellow citizens, stored artworks in the Jesuit Convent, thus saving them from destruction. In La Garriga, Mr. Llongueras brought everything he could rescue to the house of Mr. Plandiura. In Granollers, a group of volunteers took an enormous variety of objects from everywhere to an old prison. In Lérida the rescue work began when the painters, Lamolla and Creus, took most of the contents of the Seminary Museum to the municipal museum, which was controlled by Mr. Bergós and Mr. sRoca. The monastery of Poblet, which was not harmed, always remained under the direction of Mr. Toda, who also recovered works of art from neighbouring towns. Throughout Catalonia centres of conservation were formed. The inventory that accompanies this memoir gives a complementary list of collection points.

After my initial visit to Vic my first expedition, once the activities of the Barcelona group were established, was to Igualada, where they were destroying the high altar of the parish church, a very important baroque work. I was able to arrange for its elements to be preserved. The church was later converted into a market. From there I went to Anglesola, where I convinced the Committee to let us take away the two famous Romanesque reliefs, the marvellous statue of St. Saturnino and some metalwork and embroidery that had been saved. A few days later these objects were in the Barcelona Museum.

The third stop on this first trip was Cubells where there were some interesting objects which the Lleida Group collected a few days later. On the same journey I was able to examine the destruction of the town of Bellpuig where the church had been set on fire. The grandiose tomb of Folch, a 16th century Italian work in marble, and a magnificent 14th century painting had disappeared, possibly burned. In the town of Castelló de Farfaña I found boys destroying some 14th century sculpted stone *retablos*. I proposed to the *Ajuntament* that, by paying 'wages' from the *Generalitat,* these *retablos* could be dismantled and taken to the Lleida Museum instead, and this was done. On another journey I organized urgent repairs to the Monastery of Ripoll, but arrived too late to prevent the destruction of the apse of Sant Pau in the neighbouring village of Sant Joan de las Abadessas. This whole monastery was really under threat and objects were successfully removed to Barcelona. We were also able to send the Romanesque Christ in Majesty of Sant Joan les Fonts to Barcelona.

In this way I visited many towns in Catalunya over several months, directing collections, trying to help the tireless and self-sacrificing volunteers, who were sometimes real martyrs, who came out to the various villages. In the majority of cases, these poor art-lovers suffered the distrust of those who saw them as camouflaged guardians of the Church. Because of the necessary contact with revolutionary committees they were criticized by their fellow citizens who, in spite of their profound religiosity, were paralyzed with fear and only dared watch their burning churches with forced smiles on their lips . Frequently they themselves helped to destroy venerated images that had been in their homes for generations.

In some cases the 'saviours' got there ahead of us. In Cardona, for example, a group of the F.A.I. carried off the silver objects and it was only possible to rescue the gothic *retablos*. In La Bisbal the F.A.I. also seized a painting by El Greco and many silver objects. In spite of all our negotiations these objects were never recovered. In Seo de Urgel the committee was made up of miners who had nothing to do with the town. They were convinced that objects of value still remained in the Cathedral and let us move the mountains of wood stacked in the interior after the destruction of the altars. They saw that we were perfectly familiar with the interior and that below this pile there were still objects of artistic value. They thought that I was a curate in disguise and could not understand how a layperson would know about the treasures in a church in such detail! I had enormous difficulty escaping from them, but the 14th century painted tombs and a marvellous marble sculpture were saved.

oon the destructive offensive against religious buildings began again. Some churches of great interest were lost to fire in the first days; those that still stood after a month of revolution suffered a second attack, just as terrible as the first. The Committees, thanks to fines, extraordinary contributions and confiscations, had plenty of money. A large number of industries were paralysed, which added enormously to the number of people out of work. The consequence was that money was then spent to create work for the unemployed. Thus began the demolition of many churches and convents. In Manresa they had already destroyed the Church of the Carmen and were ready to demolish the Cathedral, one of the finest gothic buildings in Spain. Rubiralta telephoned me immediately and I spoke with Gassol, who communicated with the Government Council, but there was no way to prevent this destruction. As a last resort I went to talk with García Oliver. I tried with all my might to persuade him of the artistic importance of this building in Manresa and that it would be an absurd waste to demolish a building whose land had no value or possible utility. He answered that he understood this, but could not use his influence for the preservation of a church. In desperation I went to Manresa. I spoke to the Committee and proposed converting the church into a political meeting hall. I pointed out that this was the way that the Church of Notre Dame was used during the French Revolution. This idea saved the marvellous structure. Unfortunately a group of militiamen guarded it and a few months later they set fire to the organ which was still intact. In Solsona they were also talking about tearing down the Cathedral, which had already been turned into a garage and depository for the unions, as happened to so many churches in Catalonia. My tactics in this case were to direct the demolition by making them spend money taking down the structures that had been added later. These, having no artistic value, had deformed the cathedral and covered up the great 12th century structure. During this work we discovered some very notable sculptures.

In Puigcerdá the demolition advanced quickly once it had become possible to visit the town. Remember the famous Committee of Puigcerdá. It was one of the most dangerous and kept the city incommunicado for months. We succeeded in saving the tower and the gothic portal of the parish church. On this trip we discovered some extraordinarily important paintings, unknown until then, in the old Monastery of Santo Domingo, recently converted into a jail.

The big baroque church in Mataró was not only intact but also still had its big High Altar *Retablo*. I received news that its demolition was imminent and immediately visited the Committee. Continuing the ruse that had had such good results on previous occasions I suggested converting the church into an enormous concert hall. For that they could still use the organ and the baroque decoration of the altar, which would not be inappropriate in a concert hall. As always, I promised to direct the work personally but I was then so busy that it would be necessary to wait some time; I asked them to close the church for the moment. They did so and even published the notice of my visit and outline of my project in the daily papers.

After a few days, I ran into an old friend, the architect Mr. Rafols, who was high up in the administration of the Barcelona Museum. He said to me "Gudiol, one day you will pay dearly for this mania you have of transforming all our best churches into Red meeting places." The poor man did not understand the real purpose of my actions and that thanks to them irreplaceable losses were averted. I should make it clear that he always refused to participate in our rescue missions. The mentality of Mr. Rafols, a relatively cultured gentleman and author of various art books, made me understand the reason for objections to our efforts on behalf of the artistic patrimony.

The Monuments Section, once the avalanche of petitions for rescue had died down and important works from private collections were stored in the museum, began to recover works of decorative value. These included furniture, lamps and paintings from the eras of Isabel II and the Romantics. Thanks to the personal initiative and active intervention of Mr. Carbonell, who until then had been one of the anonymous collaborators in the rescue work, a storage area was set up, first in an old hospital on the Carrer de la Palla, and later also in the palace of the Duke of Solferino. Mr. Carbonell did not rest for a second during the three years of conflict; he was able to collect an enormous quantity of pieces of great interest. He listed the provenance of each. Mr. Martorell tried to impede this work but finally left Mr. Carbonell complete freedom of action.

While adapting the hospital on the Carrer de la Palla important pieces of alabaster, probably by the 15th-century sculptor Pere Oller, were discovered. When the Cathedral was handed over to the Monuments Section and once all of the *retablos* had been removed by museum personnel, its control was entrusted to Josep Bardolet, one of the volunteers who had worked on the transfer of the collections to the museum. We were also able to substitute police for the City Militia. The archives were carefully taken by a group of volunteers who worked under the direction of Mr. Durán to the Convent dels Àngels. The building had been adapted for the storage of documents. A small brigade of museum personnel continued the removal from the Cathedral of wood that might have inspired pyromaniacs. During the course of this work a magnificent *retablo* was found, the work of

Jaume Huguet (1470), which had been made into liners for benches in some of the chapels. I think that it was during the transfer of these archives that the beautiful sword of the Constable of Portugal was found. Now an order arrived to open all the tombs. We were able to postpone this although it had already been carried out in the Cathedrals of Tarragona and Gerona, in the latter under Folch i Torres. The opening of tombs in the Cathedral of Barcelona was done with great care by personnel from the Archeological Museum. The tomb of St. Eulalia contained a little wooden urn, which was photographed; it contained a few carbonized bones and decayed pieces of gothic brocaded cloth embroidered in gold with *fleurs de lis.* In the tombs of two bishops in the ambulatory some gothic wooden crosiers were found. In that of the 14th century Bishop Escales the body was found with a chasuble and crosier of archaeological interest. All these objects were carefully collected and deposited in the Chapter Room.

The Treasury had not been broken into by the unions and was still intact. After many months an order arrived to give it to the treasurer of the *Generalitat*. An inventory was taken. I took photographs of the display cases that contained the pieces from the Treasury before they were opened. A specialist removed all the jewels from the monstrance, donations from devotees over the centuries. The jewels were photographed one by one, not only those of artistic or archeological value, but also those of purely material value. The Treasury of the *Generalitat* took possession of everything after signing a detailed receipt, which remained in the hands of Mr. Martorell.

The other religious edifices of Barcelona remained under the control of a group of architects of the *Ajuntament*. They took charge of closing up their entrances so that people could not continue destructive acts of arson. These municipal architects also oversaw the reconstruction of the big gothic hall of the old Royal Palace of Barcelona in the interior of the Convent of Santa Clara, hidden under a series of modern additions.

The architect, Mr. Martorell, did not show even minimal interest in saving the artistic patrimony. His work consisted of simply making difficulties and slowing down the task of collecting objects that still remained abandoned in the towns. He was zealous only in insisting the regular budget of the *Generalitat*, the only resource that the Section of Saving the Patrimony could count on, be used to defray the expenses of this work. He spent the greater part of the budget on restoring the walls of Tarragona. Work on the Arch of Barà, the ancient ruins of Roda and other restoration was slowed down. He left the Capilla de la Sang of Alcover and other monuments to be destroyed. All could have been saved with just a little effort on his part. The groups of volunteers in the region continued to work for nothing, making real sacrifices to pay for trips and transport, taking advantage of any means and circumstances to bring to the notice of the official bodies those abandoned objects that remained in the villages. After a lot of insistence, Mr. Martorell proposed to the Culture Council some extraordinary funds but the money only started to arrive when it was too late and, even then, once it was given it was used for absurd wartime restorations. In those days, when there were so many urgent requirements, thousands and thousands of *pesetas* were spent on work in the monasteries of Santes Creus, San Cugat de Vallés and other sites that were not in the least endangered. On each of my trips I had to advance my own money for the price of petrol and lodgings and it was always very difficult to be reimbursed. The change of councillors on the Culture Committee was fatal to the artistic patrimony. In the beginning Gassol had Mr. Pont as his secretary and he did everything he could to help us. This assistance dropped to nothing or was even counterproductive under the councillors Isbert and Pi Suñer, who only bothered to mention the artistic patrimony when it proved useful for propaganda purposes.

Some regional groups secured funding from the *Ajuntament*. In Girona they were especially generous. The one in Tarragona which provided many facilities but no money secured some funding from the *Generalita* without Mr. Martorell's intervention. The group in Lleida was the poorest of all, but the most active. I still do not understand how, without the least economic aid, they were able to collect countless works of art of great interest in just a few months. Within days of receiving news of the existence of a piece in the district it would reappear safe and sound in the Lleida Museum. This activity was interrupted when Lamolla and Crous, active members of the group, were called up.

It was not only Catalonia, though, that suffered the rapid loss of its works of art: Aragon suffered even worse predations. One day some boxes full of religious metalwork, for the most part chopped up, arrived at the *Generalitat*. These boxes had been sent from Aragon. The terrible news that filtered through from time to time of fires and acts of destruction was confirmed. Inquiries were made from the militiamen returning from the Aragonese front that made clear that, as in Catalonia, the majority of the churches had been burnt or used as warehouses by the unions after their altars and furnishings had been destroyed. The sculptor Fenosa showed up one day at the *Generalitat* with a truck borrowed from the U.G.T. that was filled with *retablos*. Among them was the enormous *retablo* from Grañén and part of the one from Pallaruelo de Monegros as well as some other panels from the celebrated *retablo* of Lanaja partially burnt. They told us that owing to the lack of suitable transport rain had damaged some *retablos* recovered from Castejón de Monegros. Fenosa gave us detailed news and begged us for assistance in saving Aragonese art.

The Culture Council authorized me to visit Aragon and I left for Lleida, accompanied by the photographer Robert. In Lleida Lamolla joined the expedition. In Tamarite de Litera I received confirmation that the gothic *retablos* of the Collegiate Church, the *Patrocinio* and the churches of San Miguel and Santa Catalina had been burnt. The Romanesque Chapel of San Miguel had been demolished and its magnificent 14th century crucifix perished with it. In addition the gothic *retablos* of Algayón, Ontineña, Villanueva de Sijena, Onteñiente and Lanaja had all been burned. These irreparable losses culminated at Sijena where the famous Aragonese monastery, the royal mausoleum of Aragon, was a mountain of burned ruins. The patio doors, opened wide, revealed the magnificent Romanesque portal with its arches blackened and its doors ripped off. Both the choir of the church and the altars had been consumed by fire or reduced to splinters. We could see the half-mummified bodies of the convent's founders, Lady Sancha of Aragon and her daughter Dulce in the choir, surrounded by the bones of the Knights of Muret. By a miracle the fire had spared the wooden polychrome coffins that contained the bodies of some noble abbesses of the 15th century, whose skeletons appeared among the tombstones of the church. Hardly stopping to examine all this destruction, I ran across the ruins of the old cloister towards the famous 13th century chapter room. I could not contain my tears in front of the ashes of one of the finest monuments in the world. The very beautiful Arab *artesonado* that had covered the room's ceiling was reduced to a coating of ashes, covered by fragments of scattered roof tiles. The arches, previously resplendent with polychrome, were now a grey and black ruin that stood out against the sky. The fire had transformed the marvellous compositions, which only a few months before had seemed recently completed, into almost invisible monochromatic figures. The greater part had disappeared in the collapse of the plaster, leaving the stone walls denuded and blackened. After the shock I had felt seeing Santa Maria del Mar burned, this ruin of Sijena remains my most tragic memory of these three years of destruction.

I went to speak with the committee of Villanueva de Sijena, who handed over to us some gothic panels that had been collected from the monastery. They assured us that the arsonists were unknown, people passing through the town perhaps or the F.A.I. column of 'Eaglets,' who had burned the Cathedral of Lleida. They told me that they were ready to help me save some of the paintings in the chapter room. I promised to return soon, ready to do everything possible to ensure that what little remained should not be permanently lost and told them to remove the polychrome gothic coffins which were then sent to the Museum of Lleida together with the gothic *retablos*.

From there we went to Alcañiz. The religious buildings were intact, but their contents were totally smashed. In the castle revolutionary frenzy had resulted in the violent opening of the tomb of Lanuza, and it remained half-destroyed. By chance the chamber in the keep, decorated with magnificent 13th century paintings, was intact. In any case it was necessary to seal it to avoid people taking refuge inside, a dangerous thing for the paintings. I went to speak with the military commander of the plaza and succeeded in having the entrance closed up.

There was news that in Barbastro the military authorities, together with the revolutionary *junta* of Aragon, had tried to organize a group to save artistic patrimony and already collected some things. I therefore went to Barbastro.

This city had been converted into a military centre on the Aragon front. The churches were being used as warehouses and nothing remained of the church furnishings, among them some gothic *retablos*. I tried to examine the antique pieces which were said to be in one of the rooms of the *Ayuntamiento*, but I could not find the man with the key. During these inquiries I met an ex-professor of the Huesca Institute who said that they were trying to organize, in cooperation with the military authorities in this sector, a group to save the artistic patrimony. I worked that day and subsequently on other trips and also from Barcelona on this, but it was impossible. Aragon had no one who took care of artistic patrimony and what had survived the destructive avalanche of the fires during the first days was destroyed slowly over the next three years.

The only two hotels in Barbastro were requisitioned by the Town Committee and the military authorities and were completely full. For this reason we decided to go to Alquezar where we arrived at nightfall. We went directly to the Committee and presented our papers which were examined with suspicion. I could not figure out if the artistic treasures of the famous Collegiate Church were intact or not. They put up all sorts of obstacles before agreeing to a meeting the next morning. We went to the inn. Lamolla and I shared a room. At three in the morning we were violently awakened by a group of men armed with rifles. It was a terrifying moment. They looked at us without saying anything. They made us dress quickly and go with them. Was this the classic 'death walk'? They took us to the *Ayuntamiento*. The whole Committee was in session there and a group of militia was at the doorway. Fortunately, the ex-professor from Huesca whom we had met that morning was there and everything was explained. The Committee had thought that we were a group of antiquity robbers and urgently sent to Barbastro for a militia company. Luckily, the professor was with them as a technical advisor. Maybe this saved our lives. Without him might we have shared the fate of a group of painters who had been shot two months earlier in Huesca? The next morning we went to the Collegiate Church with the whole Committee.

Everything was there, the best objects hidden under a scene of apparent destruction, under a theatrical disorder of mountains of chairs, paintings off the walls and saints laid out on the ground. I realized immediately that all of the latter was camouflage and that the Committee was formed of good people who were afraid to show us their church that had not been burnt. We made friends, we understood each other without speaking and all the treasures of Alquezar were revealed and photographed: the two *retablos*, the cloister capitals, the silver crosses and chalices, the Romanesque crosier of Umfal. I advised them to continue to guard everything and not let anyone enter the church. I had no opportunity to return to Alquezar where one of the most frightening events of my life was compensated for by the great joy of finally finding a practically intact monument.

The town of Benabarre was our destination the following day. It was under the absolute authority of an ex-miner from Suria, who told us about the execution of the curate and the ten lawyers who, according to him, kept the town in perpetual struggle. He put at our disposal everything that had been saved of artistic value; among these things were the magnificent 16th century silver casket, various important pieces of metalwork, and the marvellous 15th century *retablo* by Jaume Ferrer.

It was necessary for me to return to Barcelona but I could not leave Aragon without knowing the fate of the famous treasure of Roda de Isábena. I left Lamolla with a list of what Roda possessed to assess what had been preserved and I went to Barcelona. I would be surprised, on returning to Lleida after a few days, to find all the Roda treasure in the Museum. Logrollo had succeeded in convincing the responsible and knowledgeable Roda Committee to send their treasures to Leida to avoid the risk of destruction. A commission of Roda citizens accompanied it to the Museum, and Mr. Roca, as director, signed a receipt for all the pieces in his care. I have a letter that the Marqués de Lozoya wrote to me, saying that the treasure of Roda had arrived safe and sound in the hands of those now reorganizing the artistic patrimony.

Once in Barcelona, I gave a full account of my activities in Aragon to Mr. Martorell, asking him at the same time to allocate 4,000 pesetas so that a technician might be sent to Sijena, to remove and carry to safety what remained of the wall paintings. I showed him photographs which indicated exactly what could be saved and the dangers to the remaining paintings which were at the mercy of the elements. Each passing day damaged more of the consistency of the polychrome already weakened by fire. I did not succeed in attracting his interest. I then went to speak with Gassol's secretary and showed him the photographs. He was impressed by my description and gave instructions to the treasurer of the *Generalitat* to release the necessary funds. I immediately left for Sijena accompanied by Robert and Llopart, who worked with great care and skill to remove the paintings in the chapter room. They were assisted by people from the town of Villanueva de Sijena. I instructed them not to remove the wall paintings in the apse because I did not believe that they were threatened. More than a year later I had the opportunity to visit the ruins of Sijena that had been converted into a stable and they were still intact.

The success of the work carried out in Sijena inspired us to continue removing mural paintings in bad condition. The first was the notable 14th century decoration that appeared beneath the modern construction over one of the altars of the parish church of Cardona. This removal was carried out by Llopart. Immediately following were the wall paintings of Osomort, which had been heavily damaged by the burning of the building, then my brother Ramon did those of Sant Martí Sescorts and Folgaroles. Afterwards both he and Llopart removed the famous paintings from the monastery of Pedret and, right after that, those of Sant Pere de Casserras. The only paintings removed were those considered immediately at risk. In this way we limited ourselves to cleaning and erecting a protective partition wall around those discovered in the old Monastery of Puigcerdá.

Then my brother and Llopart were called up. They tried to cross into France but were captured and sent to a concentration camp, where they remained until almost the end of the war. When I was also called up all the work of removing wall paintings stopped. Those of Sant Martí Sescorts, Folgaroles and Osomart were deposited in the Vic Museum. The others, along with those from Sijena, were taken to the house of Madame Teresa Amatller, at 41, Passeig de Gràcia. When she left Barcelona, she had given me her apartment to use for saving the artistic patrimony and this is what was done. A workshop was improvised there and the restorer, Mr. Navarro, under my direction, began the transfer of the paintings of Pedret, Sijena and Cardona. These last,, upon completion, were installed in the offices of the Monuments Section. If these paintings had not been removed, they would have been seriously damaged or disappeared, like those of the Esglesia de la Sangre in Alcover, where the building was demolished, and those of the Church of the Carmen in Manresa because of rain damage. For that reason, the most urgent case was that of Sijena. If they had not been taken down immediately, given the weather from the time of the collapse of the roof and the flaking of the plaster after the fire, they would have completely disappeared during the winter of 1936. The restorations were technically perfect. Some elements from Pedret were damaged, perhaps during transportation, due to a lack of materials during the last year of the war and also perhaps because I was mobilized, as my visits to Barcelona were brief and infrequent. I have to say though, that in spite of the fact that these colleagues were unpaid or worked for very little money, they performed their work with praiseworthy enthusiasm.

This work relating to the removal of mural paintings made museum personnel jealous. Folch i Torres advised me that there was gossip that I had removed the wall paintings myself. Later, I found out that he told various friends of mine that the rescue of artistic patrimony was simply in my personal interest and that someday they would see the Sijena paintings on the foreign art market. Grau, the restorer of the Museum, apparently said that the paintings had been removed by people not familiar with the proper technique. The same people who carried this out now work as restorers for the Committee for the National Artistic Patrimony, having had great success in the difficult removal of some 14th century paintings in Valladolid - paintings that Mr. Grau declared impossible to remove.

Another task that fell to me was the preparation for moving the contents of the Museum of Barcelona. Nobody thought it was necessary. This idea was purely that of Folch i Torres, who did not consider it very secure; after the campaign of the Workers' Solidarity Movement he insisted and eventually obtained an order from the Council to move everything to the museum at Olot. He put me in charge of supervising the difficult task of cutting the enormous Romanesque apses into moveable sections. This occupied days of my precious time dedicated to the salvation of many abandoned works .

Every day unknown objects were found in the most unexpected places. For example, after a few months, in a little abandoned convent in Barcelona, Camilo Bas, one of our colleagues discovered a magnificent alabaster head, a 14th century piece, and a gothic iron grille. At the same time, some of the rescuers began to give works of art to the *Generalitat*. The Painters' Union of the *Carrels dels Arcs* handed over some statues and a grille from Santa Ana and a magnificent Aragonese *retablo*. A union working out of the house of Mr. Milà on the Passeig de Gràcia, gave us some gothic *retablos* that were a part of Milà's collection. Another committee, installed in the *Casa de la Virreina*, contributed the magnificent *retablo* by Pau Vergós. In the same way, the *retablos* of the Marquis de Robert were collected, others were found in the country house of the Conde family in Prat de Llobregat, and yet others in the houses of Joaquín Carreras, Fontana, Dr. Soler, Vidal, Rusiñol, etc.

n the middle of September it was possible to establish the first state inventory of monuments and works of art that remained more or less under the control of the *Generalitat*. At any rate, there still remained an indefinite number of small towns of whose fate we did not have even the slightest information. I established an inventory of securely documented works. The Culture Council proposed publishing it in a pamphlet in order to recognize the role of the *Generalitat* in the task of protecting the artistic patrimony. A small memorandum was drawn up but its publication remained up in the air. After a few months the Propaganda Commission took the manuscript from the Culture Council and, with modifications to its preliminary text, published a pamphlet in English and French entitled *The Salvage of Catalonia's Historical and Artistic Patrimony* at the same time as the inauguration of the Exhibition of Catalan Art in Paris. This pamphlet includes the inventory that I had edited with a clear indication of all lost and burned objects and the list of artistically important churches that had been burned or otherwise destroyed, however it was generally

1936 The Sack of Santa Maria del Mar.

misunderstood. I think it was a newspaper in Brussels which published an extensive article condemning it, intimating that people who could read between the lines would see proof in it of the irreparable destruction in Catalonia. Within revolutionary circles in Barcelona this point of view was taken into consideration and I was accused of being a 'shameful Fascist'. Friends advised me that the accusation came from the same Propaganda Commission. I had to hide until the danger of the fateful 'death walk' abated.

I have also been violently accused for my collaboration in the book that *Cahiers d'Art* published in Paris in 1937 with the title *L'art de la Catalogne*. In effect I am the author of that book . I had already prepared the greater part of it before the war. On a visit that Christian Zervos, the editor of *Cahiers d'Art,* made to Barcelona he asked me for something to publish and I offered him the book, which is actually a summary notice concerning the evolution of art in Catalonia, from its origins until the formation of a united Spain. More than anything, it is a book of discovery with a very short text and many good photographic reproductions. With this material in his hands, Zervos offered the Commissary of Propaganda the publication in French of a sensational book in defence of the Republic, and thus obtained important economic aid. Once in Paris, Zervos did nothing more than publish my whole book, prefacing it with a prologue signed by him and dedicating the work to the political directors in Barcelona. This prologue is a string of falsehoods and exaggerations that constitute the basis of the accusations against the book. They printed three editions, one in French, the second in English and the third in German. The first two contain the dedication and prologue. The German edition is completely my book, just as I gave it to Zervos. I beg that it be the one judged. I am not responsible for the additions incorporated to obtain an official subvention. Two thousand copies of the German edition were sold during the war in Germany. It seems that more should be printed to demonstrate the absolute scientific spirit of my book.

It is important to realize, in defence of my collaboration in the pamphlet *The Salvage of Catalonia's Historical and Artistic Patrimony,* that the list included relating to the state of monuments and museums was copied by the Marqués de Lozoya and sent by him, in his capacity as General Sub-Commissioner of the Defense of the National Artistic Patrimony, to Dr. Walter W.S. Cook, President of the Institute of Fine Arts of New York University. I submit a photocopy.

Among the accusations levelled against me during the Spanish tragedy was my participation in the visit of the Dean of Canterbury to Barcelona, Valencia and Madrid. One day I was called to the office of the Councillor of Culture, who ordered me to accompany the Dean on a visit to the Cathedral, Pedralbes, museums and other artistic monuments in Barcelona. For an entire day I went around Barcelona with the Dean, trying to show, in every way possible, the truth of what had occurred during the period of absolute anarchy. I took him not only to visit the work carried out to save the monuments and artworks, but also to see the irreparable destruction caused by the fires. He gave me the impression that he understood the truths hidden under those burnt-out naves of Santa Maria del Mar and the thousands of paintings and furnishings stored in the museums.

The next day, the Dean was leaving for Valencia accompanied by one of the members of the Commission of Propaganda. For quite a while I had wanted to find an opportunity that would permit me, without taking up too much time, to see what our counterparts were doing in Valencia to rescue the artistic patrimony of that region. Also, it was rumoured that some treasures from the Prado Museum had been taken to Valencia. So I asked permission to be included in this expedition which was leaving by car from Barcelona. I thus had the chance to visit the city of Castellón on the way, where they were demolishing a gothic church - a deed I denounced in Valencia. Once there, I had the chance to see the stockpile of artworks in the Collegio de la Patriarca and the work they were doing at the Serrano Gate to make it into a storage facility for paintings from the Prado. When I said goodbye to the Dean in order to return to Barcelona in the car belonging to the Propaganda Commission, the Commissioner proposed continuing to Madrid. The prospect of visiting Madrid was an irresistible temptation. I accepted and rejoined the expedition, which was by car, under the direction of an employee of the Minister of Propaganda who was fluent in English. We were in Madrid for a little more than 24 hours, during which time I was only able to visit the Royal Palace and the artworks assembled in the Church of San Francisco el Grande. The Dean made several visits arranged by the Ministry of Propaganda before returning to Valencia and catching a plane to France, and I took a train back to Barcelona.

After the visit of the Dean of Canterbury, I was called on many times to serve as a guide for visiting foreigners. I tried to avoid these missions whenever possible, but in the end I realized that when the visitors praised the Organization for the Salvation of Works of Art there were benefits both for the Organization and the works of art themselves. In this way, thanks to being one of the few things being done in Barcelona that everyone could talk about, even if they had to hide their true sentiments, we began to receive more effective support from the authorities.

On another occasion I accompanied a group of archaeologists, sent by the English government to Catalonia to see the damage to artistic treasures. I took them to Montserrat, which was practically intact, and to Vic where they saw the burned Cathedral. At Olot they saw the largest collection of art in Catalonia. In Girona we visited the Cathedral and the museums. At Poblet we were received by Mr. Toda. Tarragona was the last stop, after which they went on to Valencia. As a commentary relating to that visit I suggest you read the article that Sir Frederick Kenyon, who led the commission, published in the *Times* of London.

Folch y Torres arrived in Barcelona one day and put me in charge of picking up some works of art in Lleida, Tarragona, Vic and Girona which were to be part of the exhibition that, in agreement with the *Generalitat,* he was organizing in Paris. A few days later I received a letter from Dr. Walter W.S. Cook, Chairman of the Institute of Fine Arts of New York University, announcing his visit to Europe and asking if it were possible for me to come to Paris to speak with him. After a long process, and thanks to the Exhibition of Catalan Art at the Jeu de Paume Museum, I was given a passport. I spoke with Dr. Cook, who tried to convince me not to return to Barcelona. He offered to cover my expenses if I would conduct a photographic campaign covering French

Romanesque art sponsored by the Metropolitan Museum of Art, the Frick Art Reference Library and Harvard and Princeton Universities. Unfortunately I could not accept. My wife and children were effectively hostages in Barcelona guaranteeing my return from France. I asked him to postpone the exhibition until after the war. As I will recount later, Cook kept his word. I returned to Barcelona after a few days. Awaiting me was a new role in the Spanish drama. I was mobilized. My call up might have been avoided by a simple intervention from Mr. Martorell saying my work at the Section of Monuments of the *Generalitat* was essential. Before leaving for the front I made one last expedition. Josep Bardolet and I made a quick trip to see all the churches in the Taüll and Boi Valleys to verify that the great Romanesque churches were well preserved and only the furniture had disappeared. In the end, some furniture was found stored in Lleida. To complete my service at the Monuments Section I edited a memoir of which I have the original with annotations by Mr. Martorell, advising the Culture Council of the state of the collections of artworks in Catalonia.

I completed my military service with the draft of 1925 in the Topographical Brigade of Engineers and my active service with the rank of Sergeant. Within the first months of the war all the officers and classes were called up. I did not present myself and continued working with the group saving the artistic patrimony. A few months later, the order for my mobilisation arrived at the Culture Council, advising them that there was a charge of desertion against me. I was obliged to present myself at the barracks but, thanks to a letter about the work I had been doing, I was saved from having to join a disciplinary battalion. However, in the end I couldn't avoid being called up. After much negotiation, effectively aided by the College of Architects, instead of joining the regular army I was able to obtain a position as an architect for fortifications. They sent me to Lleida and my final destination was the subsector of Gandesa, where I arrived at the beginning of October 1937. My work consisted of drawing up, with the aid of three soldiers, detailed plans of the fortification works that would protect the municipalities of Gandesa, Bot, Horta, Bates, Villala and Pobla de Masaluca. After a few months they ordered me to clear up the fortifications that had been built at the beginning of the revolution and to finish others that had been started with the aid of civilians. It was hard to find men willing to work on the fortifications and the work progressed at an extraordinarily slow rate. This long period of calm enabled me to work on my art studies. In Gandesa I wrote a book on 14th century painting. On my regular trips to Lleida I directed the installations in the museum. Big gothic images broken up during the early days of the revolution were heroically salvaged, and the stone *retablos* of Castello de Farfanya and others were also salvaged. Because I had permission to travel within my zone and neighbouring zones I was able to continue with an inventory of the losses.

In this task I was aided by Mr. Burgal who, like myself, had been called up and was in charge of the Fraga section. Together we visited most Aragonese towns. Unfortunately the artistic patrimony in the Cinca region was almost totally destroyed. I discovered unknown Romanesque wall paintings in the town of Yeso (Huesca) and 16th century panel paintings, part of the huge *retablo* of the marvellous church of Valderrobles Castle. In the same church I recognized huge compositions in oil on canvas, some in colour and others in *grisaille,* that had surely decorated the doors of the *retablo mayor,* torn into a great number of pieces. All these objects were deposited in the Paladella house in Gandesa, which had been ceded to the army to lodge the fortification engineers. I wrote several times to Barcelona, wanting to collect this cache left in Gandesa when the army retreated to Aragon. Before leaving I wrapped all the paintings carefully and left them in the Paladella house, with a big poster explaining them.

After crossing the Ebro, I was transferred to the General Command of the Army Engineers of the East in Sant Guim (Lleida). From there I was sent to Solsona and put in charge of carpentry and hardware. I remained there until the autumn of 1938. My time in Solsona allowed me to participate in the installation then being built at the Episcopal Museum. I suggested to Mr. Martorell, the General Commander of Engineers, that by utilizing the army working brigades I be permitted to protect the Romanesque portals in the region. In spite of the commissars' opposition, Col. Martorell gave me the authorization and facilities to carry out this work, so we protected the Romanesque portals of Agramunt, one of the jewels of Romanesque Spanish sculpture, and those of Cubells, an important 13th century work with costly abutting constructions. These protective coverings, made by the army and reported by me to the Monuments Section inspired them to do more themselves , for example, the tomb of St. Eulalia of Barcelona Cathedral, the *retablo mayor* of Vic Cathedral, the portal at Ripoll and some sculptures of the Catalan *Generalitat.*

Although I could seldom go to Barcelona, I never lost contact with the *Generalitat*. I always controlled the transportion to and restoration of the paintings from Sijena, Cardona, etc., at Passeig de Gràcia, 41. I also directed the removal of the paintings of Santa Maria of Terrassa, carried out by Robert, and the cleaning of the 11th-century paintings that were discovered in the church. I visited the museums of Vic and Manresa as often as possible as objects were still being stored there. The museum in Vic was under the control of Josep Bardolet for some time, well protected by a municipal employee who guarded them jealously. The artistic patrimony was under the Subsecretary of Culture, who had moved from Madrid to Valencia and from there to Barcelona, bringing an enormous artistic treasurehouse, principally integrated into the Prado Museum. The new director was completely disoriented. With only poor Martorell to advise him, he did not know what to do, despite his good intentions. Under the influence of the personnel sent by the National Commission, the museum collections were rapidly dismantled and the pieces individually wrapped, crated and taken to new collection points close to the French border. Though I was the effective director of the Vic Museum, they told me nothing about this, nor even where the works had been taken. I later learned that they were divided between big farmhouses in the foothills of the Pyrenees, in the province of Girona.

Promoted to Head of Workshops of the Engineers Command, I was sent to Manresa where, by military order, carpentry and hardware workshops had been requisitioned. There we began to build barricades for the army, destined for hospitals. In Manresa I did everything I could to reorganize workshops that had been collectivized or ransacked. I returned each one to its owner, who now became an army employee. You can ask the carpenters and toolmakers of Manresa how I behaved towards them during the last four months of the Battle of Catalonia.

A few days before the surrender of Manresa I moved the shops to Sant Feliù de Codinas and from there to Ripoll and later to Olot, where we only remained for two days. I then received an order to go with the workshop soldiers towards Molló. Then they sent me to prison in France.

I crossed the French Frontier on 7 February, 1939 and telephoned Marcel Robin, Director of Archives of the Eastern Pyrenees, who came to find me in Prat de Molló, He put me up at his house in Perpignan, waiting for the reply to a telegram that I had sent to Dr. Walter W.S. Cook, concerning the conversation we had had many months before in Paris.

JOSEP MARIA GUDIOL I RICART

Catalogue

Blasco de Grañén

Zaragoza, c. 1400 – 1459

The Crucifixion
c. 1440 – 1445

Tempera on panel
55 ¾ x 39 3/8 in. 141.5 x 100 cm

PROVENANCE:
Private Collection, France by 1936.
Sold Maître Delvaux, Drouot, Paris, 8 April 2009.

LITERATURE:
La Gazette de l'Hôtel Drouot, no. 15, 17 April 2009, Maître Jean-Marc Delvaux, p. 37.
La Gazette de l'Hôtel Drouot, no. 13, 3 April 2009, p. 30-31.
http://www.heraldodesoria.es/index.php/mod.noticias/mem.detalle/idnoticia.21077/rel 'La DGA deja escapar también la compra de una pieza lanaja subastrada en París', 24 April 2009.
http://www.diariodelaltoaragon.es/NoticiasDetalle.aspx?Id=564718 24 April 2009.
http://www.elperiodicodearagon.com/noticias/noticia.asp?pkid=489821 24 April 2009.

RELATED LITERATURE
A.A.V.V., Guía breve del Museo Lázaro Galdiano, Fundación Lázaro Galdiano, Madrid, 2005.
ABBAD RIOS, F., Catálogo monumental de España, Zaragoza, C.S.I.C., Madrid, 1957.
ALBAREDA, JOSÉ AND JOAQUIN, 'Los primitivos de la iglesia de Lanaja', *Revista Aragón*, 8, nº 125 (1936): 34-36, and nº 126 (1936): 54-56.
AMADOR DE LOS RÍOS, RODRIGO, 'El Libro Verde de Aragón,' *Revista de España*, Vol. CVI, September/October 1885, p. 255.
AMILL, C. 'Crucifixió', *Collecció de taules gòtiques de llegat Antoni Pedrol Rius*, Ajuntament de Reus, Reus, 1993. Inventory number 9504.

Fig. 13. *The Crucifixion*, The Matthiesen Gallery, London.

ARCO, R. DEL., *Catálogo Monumental de España*, Huesca, Madrid, 1942.

BARDAVÍU PONZ, V., *Historia de la AntiquísimaVilla de Albalate del Arzobispo*, Zaragoza, 1914.

BERTAUX, É., *Exposición Retrospectiva de arte, 1808-1908*, Zaragoza, París, 1910.

CABEZUDO ASTRÍAN, J. 'Nuevos documentos sobre pintores aragoneses del siglo XV', *Seminario de Arte Aragonés*, 7-8- 9, Zaragoza, 1957.

CAMÓN AZNAR, J. *Guía del Museo Lázaro Galdiano*, Fundación Lázaro Galdiano, Madrid, 1951 (second edition, 1993).

CARDEDERA, V., *Iconografía Española*, Vol. I, Madrid, 1855, nº. 38.

CIRIA, P., 'La DGA déjà escapar también la compra de una pieza del retablo de Lanaja subastada en París, *El Heraldo* (Zaragoza), April 4, 2009.

CRIADO MAINAR, J. 'El convento de San Francisco de Tarazona (Zaragoza), construcción y reforma de sus edificios medievales.' In *Aragón en la Edad Media, XIV-XV*, Homenaje a la profesora Carmen Orcástegui Gros. 49-72. Zaragoza, 1999.

DIMITROFF, KATHERINE, doctoral dissertation, *Unraveling Christ's Passion: Archbishop Dalmau de Mur, Patron and Collector, and Franco-Flemish Tapestries in Fifteenth-Century Spain,* University of Pittsburgh, 2008.

GALILEA ANTÓN, ANA, *La pintura gótica española en el Museo de Bellas Artes de Bilbao, Bilbao, Bilboko arte ederretako Museoa, S.A., 1995.*

GIMÉNEZ RUIZ, P., M. Díaz and Ma. C. Nachón González, 'El retablo de Tosos (Un retablo inédito),' *Cuadernos de Filosofía y Letras*, Serie 1, número 60, Zaragoza, 1967.

GUDIAL RICART, J., 'Pintura Gótica', *Ars Hispaniae*, Vol. 9, Plus Ultra, Madrid, 1955.

KROESEN, JUSTIN E.A., *Staging the Liturgy, The Medieval Altarpiece in the Iberian Peninsula,* Leuven & Paris, Walpole, Peeters, 2009.

LACARRA DUCAY, MA. DEL CARMEN, 'Cinco tablas del taller del pintor aragonés. Blasco de Grañén (C. 1422- 1459)', *Anuario* 1988, Estudios-Crónicas. Bilbao: Museo de Bellas Artes de Bilbao, 1989.

LACARRA DUCAY, MA. DEL CARMEN, 'Retablo de San Salvador. Iglesia parroquial de San Salvador en Ejea de los Caballeros.' In *Joyas de un Patrimonio*. 13-68. Zaragoza, 1991.

LACARRA DUCAY, MA. DEL CARMEN, 'Nuevas noticias de Blasco de Grañén, pintor de retablos (doc. 1422-1459).' *Aragón en la Edad Media XIV-XV*. Homenaje a la profesora Carmen Orcástegui Gros, Universidad de Zaragoza, Zaragoza, 1999.

LACARRA DUCAY, MA. DEL CARMEN, 'Retablo mayor de San Blas, de la Virgen de la Misericordia y de Santo Tomás Becket. Informe histórico-artístico,' In *Joyas de un Patrimonio*, III, Restauraciones de la Diputación de Zaragoza (1999-2003), Zaragoza, 2003.

LACARRA DUCAY, MA. DEL CARMEN, *Arte Gótico en el Museo de Zaragoza*, Gobierno de Aragón, Zaragoza, 2003.

LACARRA DUCAY, MA. DEL CARMEN, 'Blasco de Grañén en el Museo Lazaro Galdiano', *Revista de arte Goya*, nº 300, Madrid, 2004.

LACARRA DUCAY, MA. DEL CARMEN, *La pintura gótica aragonesa en el Museo Lázaro Galdiano*, Fundación Lázaro Galdiano, Madrid, 2004.

LACARRA DUCAY, MA. DEL CARMEN, *Blasco de Grañén, pintor de retablos (1422 - 1459)*, Institución 'Fernando el Católico', C.S.I.C, Zaragoza, 2004.

LACARRA DUCAY, MA. DEL CARMEN, 'Blasco de Grañén and Pedro García de Benabarre', *Spanish Painting*, Coll & Cortés, Madrid, 2012.

LAMBERTO DE ZARAGOZA, FR., *Teatro histórico de las iglesias del Reyno de Aragón*, Vol. 4, Pamplona, 1785.

LÁZARO, JOSÉ, *La Colección Lázaro de Madrid*, Madrid: La España Moderna, Madrid ,1926.

MAYER, AUGUST L., 'Die Sammlung D. José Lázaro Galdeano in Madrid.' 1910. *Der Cicerone*. Halbmonatsscherift für die interessen des Kunstforschers und sammlers (revista quincenal para los intereses de los investigadores y coleccionistas de arte), Leipzig, 2/ 9.

MAYER, AUGUST L., *Geschichte der spanisschen Malerei*. Leipzig, 1922.

MONREAL Y TEJADA, L. *Arte y Guerra Civil*, La Val de Osera, Huesca,1999.

ORTIZ VALERO, N., *Martín Bernat, pintor de retablos documentado en Zaragoza entre 1450 y 1505*, Institución 'Fernando el Católico', Zaragoza, 2012.

ORTIZ VALERO, N., 'Calvary', *Spanish Painting*, Coll & Cortés, Madrid, 2012.

POST, CHANDLER R. *A History of Spanish Painting*, Cambridge (USA), Harvard University Press, 1930-1966.

QUADRADO, J.MA., *Aragón en la serie: España sus monumentos y artes, su naturaleza e historia*, Barcelona, 1886.

SAGUAR QUER , CARLOS, 'Fondos Aragoneses del Museo Lázaro Galdeano', *Artigrama* no. 20, 2005.

SOBRÉ, JUDITH BERG, *Behind the Altar Table, the Development of the Spanish Painted Retablo, 1350-1500*, Columbia, Missouri, the University of Missouri Press, 1989.

VÁZQUEZ, OSCAR E., *Inventing the Art Collection; Patrons, Markets and the State in nineteenth-century Spain*, Pennsylvania State University Press, 2001.

A new Calvary by Blasco de Grañén

his is a panel painting by Blasco de Grañén, one of the most representative Aragonese Late International Gothic-style altarpiece painters during the second third of the fifteenth century. He worked in Zaragoza between 1422 and 1459, during which time he trained students and followers who assisted with his commissions. The panel analysed here (**Colour Plate p. 44 and Fig.1**) represents the biblical scene of Calvary that usually appears on the central pinnacle of fifteenth-century Aragonese altarpieces. This representation is based on the traditional iconography that shows the moment after the Crucifixion when Jesus has just died, as narrated by the four evangelists (Matthew 27: 33-38, Mark 15: 20-41, Luke 23: 33-49 and John 19: 18-37). In this scene Christ is surrounded by a number of people who played a role, either actively or passively, in the event:

> 'Those who crucified him divided up his garments by casting lots. And they sat down there in order to watch over him. Over his head they wrote the charge against him: *This is Jesus, King of the Jews*. Two thieves were also crucified with him, one to the right and the other to the left'. (Matthew 27: 33 – 35).

> 'One of them ran, and then soaked a sponge with wine vinegar and attached it to a reed, offering it to him to drink, and saying, "Let us see if Elijah comes to take him down"'. (Mark 15: 27 – 30).

> 'Together at the foot of the cross of Jesus were his mother and the sister of his mother, Mary, mother of Clopas, and Mary Magdalene. Jesus saw his mother and together with her the disciple he loved, saying to his mother, "Woman, behold your son". After the disciple said, "Behold your mother". And from that moment, the disciple took her with him'. (John 19: 28 – 30).

> 'The centurion who saw it glorified God saying, "Truly, this man was innocent"' (Luke 23:47).

The traditional representation of this event is evident in the work presented here, although there are a series of interesting variations, such as the reduction of the number of people who are featured in the scene.
At the centre of the composition, Christ is attached to the cross by three nails, and his naked torso is stained

by blood that flows out of the wounds inflicted upon him during the Passion. He wears the crown of thorns on his head and a pure white cloth tied to his waist. The artist paid special attention to the rendering of the anatomy of the body of Jesus.

Figures appear symmetrically on both sides of the cross. Accordingly, the Virgin Mary is observed fainting to the right hand side. She is a mature woman who covers her head with a black mantle and hides her hair under a white headdress that shows she is an elderly widow. Emphasis is placed on the deep red colour tunic that is partially hidden under her voluminous mantle.

Assisting the Virgin is Mary Magdalene, identified by her smooth mane of hair and her deep red mantle, looking painfully upon the Crucifixion. This composition was not very common, as Mary Magdalene is most frequently placed in the foreground kneeling at the feet of Christ. Alternatively, in those scenes that depict the holy women assisting Mary as she faints, Mary Magdalene holds the Virgin's left hand tenderly in order to soothe the pain of seeing her son die on the cross. One of the holy women stands behind them wearing a precious green mantle.

Fig. 1. Blasco de Grañén. Detail. *Calvary*. The Matthiesen Gallery, London.

To the left of Christ is Saint John, apostle and evangelist, the beloved disciple of Jesus (**Fig. 2**). He wears a beautiful deep red mantle and long light blue tunic that barely reveals his shoeless left foot. He is shown young and beardless, according to pictorial tradition, with medium length chestnut brown hair and hands interlaced in prayer. His face reveals his desperation for the death of his teacher and friend.

In the background, witnesses comment on the scene and gesture towards Jesus. They are soldiers elegantly dressed in period style, which surely the artist knew well. The entire event transpires before a barren rocky landscape.

The painting is of high quality and is in a perfect state of conservation. The colours have been applied with tempera paint, resulting in a brilliantly colourful work of art. The panel displays characteristics of the Aragonese School including dominant colours of red, green and blue with gilding that adorns the garments, background and halos of the holy persons.

The painter made reference to manuscript miniatures and contemporary tapestries in his works of art and gained influence from the circle of friends of the Archbishop of Zaragoza, Don Dalmau de Mur (1431 – 1456). The archbishop would put Blasco de Grañén in charge of many works and helped to expand his professional career.

Fig. 2. Blasco de Grañén. Detail. *Calvary*. The Matthiesen Gallery, London.

 he similarities between this panel and others of *Calvary* by Blasco de Grañén are noticeable. In many extant versions, he decreases the number of people in the composition to three or four. Important examples that should be mentioned included, the central pinnacles of the altarpieces of *Saint John the Evangelist* and (**Fig. 3**) *Saint James the Greater* in the parish church of San Pedro de Siresa (Huesca) (**Fig. 4 and 5**). These altarpieces have been attributed to Blasco de Grañen and dated between 1440 – 1445. The apostle

Fig. 3. *Calvary*. Altarpiece of Saint John the Evangelist. San Pedro de Siresa (Huesca).

Saint James was especially significant in mediæval Aragón. Pilgrims crossed one of the oldest passages in the Pyrenees mountain range at the Puerto del Palo, the old Roman route between Béarn and Zaragoza. They continued their journey along the river Subordán Aragón until it joined the Aragón River at the Puente la Reina de Jaca (Zaragoza). King Sancho el Mayor (1005 – 1035) opened new roads that were easier to cross, such as the passage of Somport and Canfranc, an entrance to the Aragón river valley where Jaca is

Fig. 4. Blasco de Grañén. *Translation of the Body of Saint James the Greater to Galicia*. Altarpiece of Saint James the Greater. San Pedro de Siresa (Huesca).

located. It is represented in a panel called *Translation of the Body of Saint James the Greater before the Palace of Queen Lupa*. This scene is one of the most painted episodes in the legends of this saint. Chandler Rathfon Post catalogued these two altarpieces in 1938,[1] although he initially attributed them to the 'Master of Lanaja.'

The same composition of Calvary can be observed in the altarpiece of the Virgin and Child from the Aragonese region of Oto (Boltaña) (**Fig. 6**)[2]. Today the altarpiece is divided between the collections of the Diocesan

Fig. 5 *Calvary*. Altarpiece of Saint James the Greater. San Pedro de Siresa (Huesca).

Fig. 6. *Calvary*. Altarpiece of the Virgin of Child. From the Hermitage of Santa Marina de Oto (Huesca) Museo de Zaragoza.

Museum of Barbastro, where the predella is kept, and the Museum of Fine Arts of Zaragoza, which has owned the main body of the altarpiece since 1941.[3]

The Comarcal Salvador Vilaseca de Reus Museum (Tarragona) holds a panel attributed to Blasco de Grañén of unknown origin that was originally part of a pinnacle (**Fig. 7**).[4] It also represents the moment of Christ's death. In particular, the image of the Virgin Mary is very similar to the same figure in the painting analysed here (**Fig. 8**).

Another panel that Post attributed to the 'Master Of Lanaja' representing *Saint Joachim and Saint Anna Driven from the Temple* is also a notable comparison. Post identified this piece, which was in a private collection in Paris, from a photo provided to him by the researcher A. Mayer.[5] It occupies the upper scene of the left vertical panel (*calle*) of the altarpiece body. That is to say, the physical construction is very similar to the panel studied here, in addition to its stylistic similarities. A small part of the altarpiece dedicated to the Virgin that is not part of the

Fig 7. *Calvary,* (detail), Museo Comarcal Salvador Vilaseca, Reus (Tarragona).

Fig. 8 Calvary, (detail), The Matthiesen Gallery, London.

predella is also kept in the parish church of Santa María la Mayor de Tosos (Zaragoza).[6] The pinnacle represents the Calvary as is conventional. Like the work analysed here, this scene also represents Christ at the centre of the composition with the Virgin Mary at his right joined by holy women and on the other side Saint John the Evangelist seated at the side of the cross. The representation of the Virgin Mary is also significant among the versions of *Calvary*, in addition to the number of people who participate in the event. Occasionally she is presented kneeling or seated with her head turned away from her son so that he cannot see her suffering. She is flanked by two female saints, who are also in the foreground of the scene but positioned to the left of Christ, gesturing to aid him or simply looking at their crucified friend with hands together in prayer.[7]

Blasco de Grañén was one of the most distinguished painters of his time. The first evidence documenting his life dates from 1422 in a series of documents made in Zaragoza that detailed his father's inheritance. Specifically, the document outlines the sale of one of his father's houses, located in the street Teresa Gil, to a livestock farmer and guardian of his sister, María, called Sancho Añano. These documents testify that they had another sister called Lucía, who was married to Domingo de Soria. He was possibly the father of Martín de Soria, Grañén's nephew, who was also a painter and was surely one of his followers. Upon Blasco de Grañén's death, Soria would complete some of his commissions.

Blasco de Grañén was married twice. His first wife was Pascula de Agraz, who made a will in 1444 clearly stating in her last wishes that she wanted to be buried in the chapel in the Convent of San Francisco de Zaragoza. His second wife, Gracia de Tena, was left in charge of directing the workshop after he died. Blasco de Grañén died between the months of August and November 1459[8]. Between these two marriages, he engaged in a failed relationship with Violante de Gurrea, daughter of Zaragoza merchant López de Gurrea. The relationship was not successful for unknown reasons. It should be noted that the age of marriage in the Middle Ages for women was usually between sixteen and twenty years old, whilst for Blanco de Grañén it was over twenty. Therefore, freedom to chose a spouse decreased as his prestige increased, given that the goal of most marriages was to achieve a better economic and familial status. Like the majority of painters of his time, Blasco de Grañén developed the equally important role of a master by hiring and teaching the trade of painting to young apprentices. In time, Grañén reached a level of fame as a painter that resulted in the need to increase his number of students and collaborators in order to complete the commissions he received. His workshop was on the Calle Mayor de Zaragoza and his followers came from different regions in Aragón and other areas of the Iberian Peninsula. His most prominent and important apprentice was his nephew Martín de Soria. However, Jaime Arnaldín, younger brother of the painter Juan Arnaldín, from the Zaragonese city of Calatuyud should also be mentioned. Jaime signed an apprentice contract for three years on 24 August 1433 with painter Pascual Ortoneda. But something did not go well and by 30 September 1435 he had gone to study with Blanco de Grañén for six years.

On 22 November 1445 one Petrico, son of Alfonso Fernández de Vilforado o de Belorado, entered into his training at Blasco de Grañén's workshop. His last documented apprentice was a boy called Miguel, son of Pedro de Balmaeda, who signed a contract on 16 August 1459.[9] The painter Pedro García, native of Benabarre (Huesca), collaborated with him on many works, and appears as a witness in a series of documents dated between 1445 and 1447.[10]

Blasco de Grañén worked on twenty-three altarpieces in three Aragonese provinces. From all these works, one complete altarpiece and five fragments are known and firmly attributed. The rest do not have documentation, but they are attributed to the painter for stylistic and technical reasons. The altarpiece that is completely preserved is behind the main altar of the Church of San Salvador in Ejea de los Caballeros (Zaragoza). It was a magnificent work that was unfinished when the painter died in the autumn of 1459. His widow, Gracia de Tena, had to give the task of completing the project to his nephew and follower, Martín de Soria (doc. Zaragoza 1449 – 1487).

On 24 March 1434 the vicar of the parish of San Salvador de Eleja bequeathed a few houses so that with their sale an altarpiece could be created. The contract has not been found but a series of letters of payment issued to Blasco de Grañén and later to his widow survive, in which a series of monetary sums are cited as payment.[11] The gothic altarpiece was divided into several parts: seven openings for panels in the predella, lateral wings of three vertical panels each, a central body with the image of Christ as Saviour, the pinnacles and the wooden dust guards (*guardapolvo*). The altarpiece was also designed with a gilt frame. In the central body there was a niche intended for a statue dedicated to the church's titular figure, a beautiful polychrome wood sculpture by the brothers Domingo and Mateo Sariñena. The best examples of the altarpieces that are fragmentarily preserved and have documentation should also be cited. The Museum of Fine Arts in Zaragoza preserves two scenes from the main altar intended for the church of Lanaja (Huesca)[12] The last mention of this altarpiece is a letter of payment granted to Blasco de Grañén on 7 June 1437 for 100 florins, out of the 324 that were promised to him.

Fig. 9. Blasco de Grañén. Detail. Mary, Queen of Heaven. From Albalate del Arzobispo (Teruel). Museo de Zaragoza.

The paintings that represent the Annunciation or Saint Anne or The Epiphany were deposited in the Museum of Fine Arts in Zaragoza after the Spanish Civil War.[13] The central panel of the main altarpiece of the Church of Santa María Mayor in Albalate del Arzobispo (Teruel) from 1437 has also been preserved.[14] It is a beautiful panel painting depicting the Virgin Mary seated on a throne crowned as Queen of Heaven. The child Jesus is seated on her left knee and she holds a spring of lilies in her right hand, the symbol of her virginity. The child gives a blessing with his right hand and holds an orb topped by a cross in his left. At the sides of the throne nineteen angels play musical instruments, whilst two others hold a canopy over the throne. According to Manuel Trens, 'the Virgin in Majesty is above all an apotheosis of divine maternity and humanity of the Virgin, accompanied by musical angels. But Mary is never separated from her son. Homage to the angelic hierarchies first comes by means of songs and music. Angels play the score written on separate phylacteries, scrolls or books. Sometimes they use all kinds of instruments: a portable organ, trumpets, harps, violas, lyres-harps, lutes.' [15]

A half-figure of an angel holding the shield of Archbishop Dalmau de Mur (1431 – 1456),[16] a great benefactor of the arts, appears in the foreground of this scene (**Fig. 9**). Grañén repeated the same theme in other altarpieces like those of Lanaja, Tarazona, and Ontineña. The dedicated central panel of an altarpiece commissioned by Don Luis de Santa Fe is preserved in the Museo Lázaro Galdiano in Madrid. Don Luis was the son of the deceased Esperandeu de Santa Fe, and this work was intended for the family chapel in the church of the convent of San Francisco de Tarazona (Zaragoza).[17] The three panels from the same work have been kept in the town hall of the city since 1955. Two are from the predella, one representing the Arrest of Christ and the other depicting the Washing of Pilate's Hands and the Flagellation as a double scene in the same panel. In these examples, we can undoubtedly observe the style of Blasco de Grañén, in addition to similarities with the altarpieces of Lanaja and Ontiñena.

rañén also worked for the confraternity of San Martín to execute an altarpiece in 1445 for the chapel of the brotherhood in the church of Santa Engracia de Zaragoza. Three years later, specifically 13 March 1448, he received a commission for another work for the Church of San Francisco de Borja and on 1 July 1450 he signed the agreement for the main altar of the parish church of Ainzón (Zaragoza) dedicated to Nuestra Señora de la Piedad or Misericordia, neither of which are extant.

Although a lack of documentation prohibits firm attribution, the magnificent altarpiece dedicated to Saint Blaise, the Virgin of Misericordia and Saint Thomas à Becket, currently in the parish church of Anento (Zaragoza) should also be examined for the style and technique of Blasco de Grañén's workshop.[18] It is a large altarpiece - the predella contains eleven panel openings and the central body has nine panels. Three large panels are located in the central body, whilst the side vertical parts of the altarpiece are smaller and contain three panels each. The altarpiece is surrounded by a *guardapolvo* (dust guard). The predella depicts the *Passion and Death of Christ*. Blasco de Grañén varied his iconographic models very little for these compositions, and they are repeated in many of his altarpieces. The rest of the panels depict scenes dedicated to titular saints. The right part of the altarpiece displays the legend of Saint Thomas à Becket, or of Canterbury, a subject not commonly depicted in mediæval Spanish altarpieces. Born in London on 11 December 1120, son of a rich businessman, Thomas à Becket was canonized by Pope Alexander III on 21 February 1173, three years after his death. His devotion crossed into Spain through Queen Eleanor, daughter of Henry II of England and wife of Alfonso III of Aragón (1285 – 1291). He is depicted in this scene with a beautiful golden cross in his left hand whilst the right holds a large book bound with a red cover.

The panel representing the Virgin of Mercy (*Misericordia*) is also notable (**Fig. 10**). It is an excellent painting of the figure of Mary, who faces frontally with her arms extended wide and a mantle over her arms in the centre of the composition. A pair of angels, located in the upper part of the scene holds the mantle in such a way that leaves visible all of the people who pray to her on their knees at the foot of the Virgin. She wears a beautiful long tunic of brocaded gold fitted with a girdle. A blue mantle covers her.

According to Manuel Trens, the Virgin of Mercy took on ever-greater significance throughout the Middle Ages. Although at first this image was pictured as the exclusive refuge of the clergy and later confraternities, it began to take on significance in the fifteenth century for the general public. This figure became *Mater Omnium*, the Mother of All, who protects all of humanity under her mantle.[19] Perdrizet,[20] in his book on the Virgin of Mercy, argued for the increasing popularity of this iconography in European painting during

the fourteenth and fifteenth centuries given the plague epidemics that contributed to many deaths throughout mediæval Europe. The Kingdom of Aragón, and therefore the city of Zaragoza, was not exempt from these terrible plagues. Perhaps for this reason, the fourteenth century Aragonese School provides several examples of panel paintings with this subject. These include the Altarpiece of Saint Peter the Apostle in the church of Langa del Castillo, Zaragoza, (c. 1418 – 1425). This work presents the Virgin of Mercy in a cycle dedicated to the life of the Virgin Mary on the lateral right side of the central body of the altarpiece. The same iconography is presented on the titular panel of the altarpiece of the Hermitage of the Virgen de la Carrasca de Blancas (Teruel), now kept in the National Art Museum of Cataluñya in Barcelona, created by Banant Zahortiga around 1430.

The Diocesan Museum of Teruel has a beautiful panel painting of the same subject, whose author is known as the 'Master of Teruel'. It is a work from the first half of the fifteenth century in the later International Gothic style. Blasco del Grañén repeats the same composition on the altarpiece from Ainzón (Zaragoza). The contract for this work indicates that a 'Santa Maria de Piedad' is represented in the central panel. This subject would also be used by the Hispano-Flemish style painters Martin Bernat and Bartolomé Bermejo for the central panel of the altarpiece dedicated to the Virgin of Mercy

Fig. 10. Blasco de Grañén. *Virgin of Mercy*.
Main altar of Aneto (Zaragoza).

in the private chapel of merchant Don Juan de Lobera in the cloister of the Church of Santa Maria la Mayor in Zaragoza begun in 1479 (**Fig. 11**). Years later, in 1493, Bernat created another altarpiece for the chapel of Canon Antón Talavera in the Cathedral of Tarazona (Zaragoza), which depicted the same subject in the central scene. [21]

Following fifteenth-century tradition, the praying figures underneath the Virgin are divided into two groups: the clergy and the laity. The clergy, located on the right of the Virgin, are headed by the Pope in the foreground, who can be identified by the papal tiara that covers his head and pluvial cape. Together with the other ecclesiastics, the cardinals are identified by their red capes. To the left of the Virgin Mary, located among the laity, appears the emperor wearing his standard imperial attire and the Triple Crown. At the side of the king there are also crowned nobles.

Returning to the large altarpiece from Anento, we can also mention that shields in the form of a losange displaying the arms of the King of Aragón, the Archbishop Francisco Clemente Capera (1415 – 1419) and, again, Archbishop Dalmau de Mur y Cervelló appear on the dust guard. They were possibly patrons of the altarpiece, given the splendid quality of this work.

Fig. 11. Bartolomé Bermejo and Martín Bernat. *Virgin of Mercy*, 1479. Altarpiece of the Virgin of Mercy. Grand Rapids Art Museum, Michigan, United States of America

Fig. 12. Blasco de Grañén. *Tomb of Doña María Jiménez Cornel* (+1365). From the Monastery of Santa María Sijena (Huesca). Museum of Zaragoza.

Blasco de Grañén also fulfilled other commissions, such as the tomb of Doña María Jiménez Cornel (+1355) (**Fig. 12**). This tomb from the church of the Monastery of Santa María de Sijena (Huesca) is the only example in Aragón of polychrome wooden tombs. It came to the Museum of Zaragoza in 1922.[22] He also made a triptych for the parish church of Belchite (Zaragoza) dated to 1439, which was unfortunately destroyed during the Spanish Civil War in 1936. An inscription appeared that identifies the patrons: [23]

> 'This altarpiece has been made by the honourable Pascual Bernat and Pedro Bernat in honour of the Holy Mary. Year MCCCCXXXVIII (1438)' Close to this site is the town of Albortón, where Blasco de Grañén made an altarpiece begun in 1445.

It decorated the Casa de la Diputación del Reino in Zaragoza, one of the most prestigious mediæval buildings in the Kingdom of Aragón. During the War of Independence in the second siege of Zaragoza, it was destroyed by fire on 27 January 1809. Blasco de Grañén received a letter of payment 28 August 1477 by the administrator Don Juan de Salvert for 130 sueldos. According to this document, Grañén painted two flags of royal arms located at the top of the turrets, two banners with the cross of Saint George and retouched the metal roofs of two small towers on the building. [24]

As with many other fourteenth-century painters, the treatment of faces was one of the most personal and original characteristics that defined the style of Blasco de Grañén. In addition, his interpretations always paid attention to the social status of the people shown by the variety of clothes represented, and always followed the style of the period.

There is no doubt that the workshop of Blasco de Grañén was one of the most active and important in the city of Zaragoza during the second third of the fifteenth century and that it played a significant role in the region of Aragón during this time.

NURIA ORTIZ VALERO

1. Post, Chandler R., *A History of Spanish Painting*. Harvard University Press, Cambridge, Massachusetts, vol. VII, pp. 802-804, figs. 311-312. Lacarra Ducay, M.C., *Blasco de Grañén, pintor de retablos (1422-1459)*, Institución 'Fernando el Católico', C.S.I.C, Zaragoza, 2004, p. 173.

2. Arco, R. del., *Catálogo Monumental de España*, Huesca, Madrid, 1942, p.277. Op. Cit., Post, Ch.R., vol. 3, 1930, p. 332. Op.Cit., Lacarra Ducay, M.C., 2004, p. 154.

3. LACARRA DUCAY, MC., *Arte Gótico en el Museo de Zaragoza*, Gobierno de Aragón, Zaragoza, 2003, p. 37-39.

4. Op. Cit., Post, Ch.R., vol. II, (1930), pp. 389-390, and vol. 6 (1935), p. 812; Amil, C., *'Crucifixió', Collecció de taules gòtiques de llegat Antoni Pedrol Rius, Ajuntament de Reus*, 1993, pp. 58-59. Inventory number, 9504. Op.Cit., Lacarra Ducay, MC., 2004, p. 188.

5. It was auctioned by Tajan, *Taleaux anciens*, 37, rue des Mathurins, París, 25 June 2003. Op. Cit., Post, Ch. R. vol. 8, pp. 664-669.

6. Abbad Rios, F., *Catálogo monumental de España*, Zaragoza, Madrid, C.S.I.C., 1957, p. 450. Giménz Ruiz, P., M. Díaz, and Nachón González, Ma. C., *El retablo de Tosos (Un retablo inédito)*, Cuadernos de Filosofía y Letras, 1/ 60 Zaragoza, 1967. Op.Cit., Lacarra Ducay, MC., 2004, p. 190.

7. Ortiz Valero, N., *Martín Bernat, pintor de retablos documentado en Zaragoza entre 1450 y 1505*, Institución 'Fernando el Católico', Zaragoza, 2012, p. 197-198 and Calvary, *Spanish Painting*, Coll & Cortés, Madrid, 2012, pp. 36-43.

8. Op.Cit., Lacarra Ducay, M.C., 2004, pp.11-13.

9. Op.Cit., Lacarra Ducay, 2004. pp.19-21.

10. Ibid., docs: 41,42, 46. Lacarra Ducay, M.C., 'Blasco de Grañén and Pedro García de Benabarre', *Spanish Painting*, Coll & Cortés, Madrid, 2012, pp.12-18.

11. Lacarra Ducay, M.C., 'Nuevas noticias sobre Martín de Soria pintor de retablos (1449-1487)', *Artigrama*, 2 (1985): 23-46. 'Retablo de San Salvador. Iglesia parroquial de San Salvador en Ejea de los Caballeros' in *Joyas de un Patrimonio*, Diputación de Zaragoza, Arzobispado de Zaragoza, Obispado de Tarazona, Zaragoza, 1991, pp. 13-68.

12. Albareda, José and Joaquin, 'Los primitivos de la iglesia de Lanaja', *Revista Aragón* 12/ 125 (1936): 34-36, n°. 126

(1936): 54-56, Op. Cit., Lacarra Ducay, M.C., 2004, p. 28.

13. Op. Cit., Post, Ch. R., Vol. 3, 1930, pp. 333-334. Op.Cit., Lacarra Ducay, M.C., 2003, pp. 42-46.

14. Bardavíu Ponz, V. *Historia de la Antiquísima Villa de Albalate del Arzobispo*, Zaragoza, 1914, p. 127. Op. Cit., Post, Ch. R., Vol. 3, 1930, pp. 212 - 216, figs. 333-334. Lacarra Ducay, MC., 'Nuevas noticias de Blasco de Grañén, pintor de retablo', in *Aragón en la Edad Media, XIV-XV*, Homenaje a la profesora Carmen Orcástegui Gros, Zaragoza, 1999, vol. 2, pp. 814-815. Op.Cit., Lacarra Ducay, MC., 2003, pp. 39-42. Op. Cit., Lacarra Ducay., MC., 2004, p. 24 – 27.

15. Trens, M. *María, Iconografía de la Virgen en el Arte Español*, Ed. Plus-Ultra, Madrid, 1946, pp.413-414. Ortiz Valero, N., 2014, pp. 166, 215-218.

16. Lamberto de Zaragoza, Fr. *Teatro histórico de las iglesias del Reyno de Aragón*, Tomo IV, Pamplona, 1785, p.46.

17. Camón Aznar, J. *Guía del Museo Lázaro Galdiano*, Fundación Lázaro Galdiano, Madrid, 1951 (second edition, 1993); Criado Mainar, J., 'El convento de San Francisco de Tarazona (Zaragoza), construcción y reforma de sus edificios medievales', in *Aragón en la Edad Media, XIV-XV*, Homenaje a la profesora Carmen Orcástegui Gros, Universidad de Zaragoza, Facultad de Filosofía y Letras, Zaragoza, 1999, pp. 49-72. Op. Cit., Lacarra Ducay, M.C., 2004, p.37.

18. Cabezudo Astraín, J., 'Nuevos documentos sobre pintores aragoneses del siglo X', *Seminario de Arte Aragonés*, 7-8-9, 1957, p. 69. Op. Cit., Post, Ch. R., Vol. 4, 624 – 626. Fig. 255; Lacarra Ducay, M.C., 'Retablo mayor de San Blas, de la Virgen de la Misericordia y de Santo Tomás Becket. Informe histórico-artístic', *Joyas de un Patrimonio*, III, Restauraciones de la Diputación de Zaragoza (1999-2003), 2003, Zaragoza, pp. 27-53. Op.Cit., Lacarra Ducay, M.C., 2004, pp. 111 - 154.

19. Trens, M., 1946, pp. 274-275.

20. See the work of Paul Pedrizet, in which he describes '*La Vierge, dressée dans un grand élan, invoque son fils. Des angelots font flotter son manteau, quí semble une toile emporteé por le vent*' In *La Vierge de Miséricorde: étude d'un thème iconographique*, Ed. A Fontemoing, 1908, pp. 137-159 and p. 201.

21. Ortiz Valero, N., 2014, pp. 96-100.

22. Cardedera, V., 'Iconografía Española', VoI. 1, Madrid, 1855, nº. 38; Quadrado, J. Ma., *Aragón en la serie: España sus monumentos y artes, su naturaleza e historia*, Barcelona 1886, Chapter 2., pp. 120-121. .V.V., *Boletín del Museo Provincial de Bellas Artes,* nº.6, January, 1922, 'Crónica del Museo', p. 35. Op. Cit., Lacarra Ducay, M.C., 2003, pp. 46-49. Op.Cit., Lacarra Ducay, M.C., 2004, pp.166 - 170.

23. Bertaux, É., Exposición Retrospectiva de arte, 1808-1908, Zaragoza, París, 1910, pp.49-51. Post Ch. R., 1930, vol. 3, pp. 210-212; Monreal y Tejada, L., *Arte y Guerra Civil*, Huesca, La Val de Osera, 1999, p. 28. Op. Cit., Lacarra Ducay, M.C., 2004, pp. 170 - 173.

24. Op.Cit., Lacarra Ducay, M.C., 2004, pp.108-109.

Blasco de Grañén, his shop and a Crucifixion

hrist on the Cross is by far the most frequently encountered theme in 15th-century Spanish imagery, whether painted, carved and polychrome in wood or cast in metal. A crucifix was an obligatory piece of church furniture on any altar during the celebration of mass. Crucifixes were carried in religious processions and painted or sculpted examples were to be found at the very top of every multi-paneled *retablo* or altarpiece, especially in the region of the Kingdom of Aragon (Aragon, Catalonia, Valencia and the Balearic Islands).

Many of the polychrome sculpted works for altarpieces carried a streamlined iconography: Christ on the cross with the mourning figures of the Virgin Mary and St. John the Evangelist to either side. Other paintings told the complete narrative, replete with sanctified mourners, Roman soldiers including the repentant Longinus and sometimes the two other crucified thieves as well.

The painted example by Blasco de Grañén shown here falls in-between (**Fig. 13**). A rather small Jesus is fastened with bent nails to the cross occupying centre stage; the Virgin Mary, fainting, is sustained by a saintly female and another cloaked, haloed figure with his back turned and to the right.[1] To his left (the sinister side) are three Roman soldiers, dressed as contemporary mercenaries. The soldier pointing to the cross is probably Longinus, who recognized Jesus as the Son of God. In front of these men stands the young St. John the Evangelist, hands clasped in mourning, wearing biblical robes. All these figures occupy a desolate landscape - more like a stage-set than anything else. Behind everything is a gilded sky.

This painted panel is not an isolated icon but an expected and integrated part of the larger scheme of the *retablo* and it occupied a set position. Spanish *retablos* ranged from the mid-sized for small chapels, up to the colossal in scale for high altars. These were called *retablos mayores* and often completely filled the main apse of a church. They generally consisted of a wide central *calle,* or vertical zone, with its largest image, a formal one of the saint to whom the altarpiece was dedicated, forming the liturgical centre. Placed over the principal effigy

Fig. 13. *The Crucifixion*, The Matthiesen Gallery, London.

was the Crucifixion, smaller than, but often as wide as, the main image.[2] Surrounding it would have been tiers of narrative scenes giving details of the life of the central saint. This constituted the body of the *retablo*. It in turn rested on a *banco*, a horizontal strip as wide as the body, also painted with smaller scenes generally depicting either episodes from Christ's Passion (whatever the main topic of the *retablo*) or images of other saints, usually determined by the patron. If the altarpiece were for a chapel, the centre of the *banco*, lining up with the main image and *Crucifixion*, would contain the dead Christ in his tomb; if the work were for the high altar, this position would be occupied by a gilded wooden tabernacle, a repository for the consecrated reserve host wafers. Lavish gilded frames were placed around each painted panel, usually arched in the lower tiers, and with pointed frames called *chambranas* crowning the upper tiers. In elaborate *retablos* there might also be *tubas* or *linternas*, projecting canopies of tracery. The entire body would be surrounded with framing *guardapolvos* or dustguards, tilted slightly inwards, generally adorned with the coats of arms of the people who had paid for the altarpiece, and sometimes also smaller images of saints. To understand the individual elements you had to see the whole colourful ensemble: central images for contemplation and a reminder of the eucharistic nature of the mass, side narratives for education, particularly when many parishioners could not read or write.[3]

When faced with an isolated *Crucifixion* from this time and place, if its location of origin is not known and documentation concerning it does not exist, it can be extremely difficult to identify its original context unless it was located at the top of an altarpiece. The identity of the master and workshop that produced the present piece is known and it was certainly part of a much larger construction, probably done by the most prestigious *retablo* firm in the Aragonese city of Zaragoza during the second third of the 15th century.

The master painter was Blasco de Grañén, who worked in Zaragoza from 1422 until his death in 1459.[4] Much documentation about Blasco survives. Contracts or payments still exist for at least 24 altarpieces, many vast in scale, plus painted coffins, painted curtains and painted draperies for funerals.[5] In addition, there are many undocumented works, identifiable by style, attributed both by María Carmen Lacarra Ducay and, earlier, under the name of the 'Master of Lanaja', by Chandler R. Post who died 25 years before the painter's true identity was known.[6]

Documents have revealed that over his career Blasco employed a number of apprentices, many from other regional families of painters (including Miguel Vallés, Jaime Arnaldín, and Miguel de Balmaseda), and he probably trained his nephew Martín de Soria who succeeded him. In addition, he collaborated with other master painters, a frequent practice in late-mediæval Aragon, including Jaime Romeu. He was also a witness to legal transactions relating to other masters, including Pascual Ortoneda and Pere García de Benabarre. All of this is evidence of the close professional and dynastic relations in the art world in Aragon at this time, although he sent his own son, Bernardo, to Barcelona to be apprenticed to the even more sophisticated painter, Bernat Martorell.[7]

Since several commissions were normally worked on at the same time, Blasco must have been running a virtual factory, employing assistants as well as apprentices and gilders, and either kept a carpenter on hand or subcontracted.[8] Individual panels were often quite large and heavy, constructed with well-seasoned boards glued together and supported by bars on the back smoothed down to uniformity. The preparation and painting took considerable energy and physical strength. Coats of gesso, both rough and smooth, and gilding were generally applied before painting. The medium itself was normally tempera, the colours ground in the shop and mixed with an egg-yolk binder (or other binders such as glue for certain hues). Just coming into fashion in Blasco's time was the incorporation, in many of the biggest formal images, of *embutido* which means 'stuffed' : modelled and stamped borders and adornments of raised and gilded gesso making the brightly painted surfaces even richer. The frames were made by the carpenters and then gilded. Architectural in nature they replicated the stone tracery designs in the architecture surrounding the *retablo* and, in documents, even shared the same terminology for specific decorative parts. Grañén and his workshop produced extremely large *retablos,* not only for churches in the city of Zaragoza, but also for parish churches and convents all over Aragonese territory, particularly in what today constitutes the provinces of Zaragoza, Huesca and probably neighboring Teruel as well.

Transport and installation, particularly to distant or remote locations, also offered challenges. The individual panels and framing elements, covered in sheets, would be loaded onto a mule train and a shop employee or a crew of them would travel to the site to fasten each weighty panel into place and then nail on the framing elements.[9]

These constructions were made to be durable, the colours very bright and the gilded details highly burnished in order to be seen illuminated by whatever windows, candles and oil lamps their sanctuaries possessed. Though so many *retablos* have been divided, damaged and destroyed over the centuries, many have survived as an ensemble remarkably well.

n impressive example by Blasco and his workshop, which, though undocumented, contains all the elements and the painting style of his production, survives in the small town of Anento (Fig. 14). The reason for its virtually intact state probably lies in the fact that until late in the 20th century the town was accessible only by footpath along a rocky riverbed.[10]

Since the apse of its church, dedicated to St. Blaise, is flat, the *retablo mayor* was made to occupy the entire space and is stepped at the top to accommodate to the vaulting. There is unusual variety here in the size of individual images and narratives within their *calles* to accommodate the spatial variations of the apse and its large dimensions. The altarpiece bears a triple dedication to the Virgin of Mercy, St. Blaise and Thomas à Becket with three large images, each surrounded and surmounted by narratives. It is one of the few high altarpieces that still retains its gothic carved and gilded tabernacle in the centre of its *banco,* which is flanked on either side by five scenes of Christ's passion.[11] The coats of arms of two archbishops of Zaragoza are incorporated, Francisco Clemente Çapera (1415 – 1419 and again in 1429) and Dalmau de Mur i Cervelló (1431-1456). Scholars assume that most of the work was done during Dalmau de Mur's tenure.[12] Given the limited size and remoteness of Anento, the endowment of such a large work must have been due to its donors.[13] Dalmau de Mur was a prodigious art patron ordering and financing works for both cities and countryside during his long career. The Anento retable was not the only work he would order from Blasco de Grañén's workshop.[14]

The painting seems to have been executed by several people, with consequent variations in quality and ability in the individual panels,[15] although the overall effect is dazzling and recent cleaning has revealed its overall high quality of workmanship.[16] Due to the altarpiece's vast size, most worshippers would not have been able to see the upper panels in detail and Lacarra remarks that the second horizontal tier in the *retablo's* body shows less quality than the *banco* and the larger images and narratives on the first tier.[17] This was not unusual in these large altarpieces where the best workmanship and colours were often reserved for those portions closest to the viewer. The largest images of the *retablo's* dedicated saints are brilliant examples of the great formal sweep typical of such effigies throughout the career of the Blasco de Grañén workshop. The surface-oriented juxtaposition of multiple patterns provides reinforcement to the virtual carpet of painting that characterises the whole production.

However 21st. century taste may judge the painting of the high altarpiece of Anento, Blasco Grañén's contemporaries thought he was just fine - indeed better than merely fine. He was able to ask very high prices for his large works, up to a colossal 10,000 *sueldos* for the *retablo mayor* for the church of San Salvador in Egea

Fig. 14. Blasco de Grañén & Co. *Retablo Mayor*, Anento

de los Caballeros for which he was commissioned in 1438 - a sum so large for the time that the parishioners who were financing it had trouble in meeting payment deadlines and the work wasn't completed until 1476, long after Grañén's death, by his successor, Martín de Soria.[18]

Fig. 15. Blasco de Grañén. Central panel from the Albalate del Arzobispo Retable.

any of the altarpieces both he and his studio worked on were dedicated to the Virgin Mary, not surprising in the case of high altar *retablos* since many churches were consecrated to her at this time. Given the vast dimensions of many of these works, it is not surprising to find the same narrative scenes repeated over and over with the emphasis on clarity of story-telling. The workshop must have had a collection of basic compositions with set characters for each tale, though they took pains to make special variations in each perhaps to keep themselves from getting bored with the seemingly endless repetitions. This is probably even more true of the crowning panels of the *Crucifixion* in each altarpiece, no matter which saint held the main dedication.[19]

For the large central effigies of the Virgin Mary, Grañén developed a prototype that proved very popular. Since the individual patron or group of patrons had the final choice in the approval of the finished product, it proved a successful template.

This was particularly evident between 1437 and 1439. Perhaps the best example is a panel now in the Museo de Bellas Artes in Zaragoza, which constituted the centre of an altarpiece commissioned by city officials and citizens of the town of Albalate del Arzobispo in 1437 and completed two years later (**Fig.15**). The archbishop was once again Dalmau de Mur, whose coat of arms appears in the surviving central panel. This work too was relatively costly for the time at 6000 *sueldos*. The details of the contract have not survived and presumably the narrative and *banco* panels are long gone but the central panel was moved from the parish church to that of San José in the same city sometime before 1914.[20]

The remarkable thing about this panel of the Virgin and Child with eleven angels, eight of them playing contemporary musical instruments, is that it still makes an impressive stand-alone composition and serves as the ensemble's focal point. The Virgin, dressed in traditional colours, a red dress and blue brocade mantle which is now darkened almost to black with a white ermine lining, sits on an elaborate throne. Her cloak has a border of gilded *embutido* with green accents and her crown and halo and the Christ Child's halo are also of richly patterned *embutido,* while the angels have flat gilded haloes. There is more gold in the brocade background and *embutido* highlights pick out the coat of arms of Dalmau de Mur, held by another angel. The Christ Child wears a purple robe and a sprig of coral around his neck. He blesses with one hand and holds an orb in the other. There is an apocalyptic reference in the twelve gold stars that surround his mother's halo.

All of these elements are standard Virgin and Child iconography of the period. What makes the image so impressive is its symmetry with the throne framing the Virgin and Child, like an even larger more splendid halo, the broad surfaces of painting and patterning in the grounds, brocades and the positioning of the figures themselves. The *embutido* tends to emphasize surface over depth; to modern eyes it is almost an abstraction of patterns but it is the perfect foil to bring the eye back to the surface of the ensemble. In a large *retablo* a strong emphasis on depth in so many diverse panels, be they formal effigies as here or more complex narratives, would be lethal in the context of the whole - rather like a window of many panes with a different scene and view in each. Here, the effect is of a magnificent screen and Grañén and his shop had developed the perfect synergy between formal image and narrative. It is ideal for the *retablo* format.

The template for the Virgin and Child image of Albalate proved so popular that the workshop used it on at least three other occasions in differing situations within a two-year period. Once it was employed in a *retablo* for a private patron in a monastery chapel in the Convent of San Francisco in the city of Tarazona. The chapel, the last on the left of the nave, was dedicated to Our Lady of the Angels.[21] Its patron bore the unlikely name of Esperandeu de Santa Fe, which translates roughly as 'Waiting for God of the Holy Faith'.[22] Esperandeu was not born with this name: he was originally Ezequiel or Ezmel Azanel and came from a wealthy Jewish family, one of the most prominent merchant clans of Tarazona.[23] He converted in 1413/14, convinced by Christian arguments at the disputations taking place in Tortosa between Christians and Jews.[24] For the new

Fig. 16. Blasco de Grañén. *Esperandeu de Santa Fe Retable*.

convert there was an enticement as well: he was made a knight, given the exalted prefix *Mosén* to use before his name, and allowed to wear the spurs of nobility.

He is depicted thus in the central panel of his *retablo* (**Fig. 16**), kneeling at the foot of Christ and the Virgin with an angel at lower left holding his recently designed coat of arms (a hand holding a cross of Lorraine). The inscription in the centre reads *The very honorable Mosén Sperandeu de Sancta Fe had this retablo made in honour of the glorious Virgin Mary, and it was completed in the year fourteen thirty-nine*. It is a public statement of his Christianity. This panel is now in the Museo Lázaro Galdeano in Madrid. The Virgin and Christ Child are in almost identical poses to the ones from Albalate but in even brighter colours, once more with lavish accents in *embutido*. Here there are only six angels, four playing instruments, probably because the donor and his inscriptions and emblems take up so much space. Perhaps appropriately for a patron who was also a convert, there are no gold stars around the Virgin's halo. Perhaps he did not yet want to consider the concept of the Apocalypse.

The original *retablo* was again quite large. The contract calls for 15 panels, nine narratives of the life of the Virgin (presumably the central panel was one of these), plus five in the *banco* of Christ's passion. Though the *Crucifixion* isn't mentioned, it probably constituted the fifteenth panel since the other scenes would have had to be of an even number for symmetry. It was commissioned in 1438 and completed the year after.[25]

There is no information on when the Albalate *retablo* was taken down and divided but it is possible to make an assumption about Esperandeu de Santa Fe's. In 1835, Isabel II's Liberal prime minister, Juan Álvaro Mendizábal published a proclamation of *desamortización*, the secularizing and selling off monasteries and convents with less than twelve members in order to raise money for the wars against the Carlist pretenders to the throne.[26] Although this was ostensibly justified by dividing some of Spain's considerable monastic properties between small farmers, the eventual beneficiaries were generally wealthy. The edict led not only to the dissolution of many monasteries that had flourished for centuries, but also to outright plunder. It was then that many monastic *retablos* were confiscated, cut up and sold. Like the monasteries' properties themselves, many went into the private holdings and collections of the aristocracy and, in industrial cities like Barcelona, the growing bourgeoisie.[27]

After the *desamortización*, the convent complex of San Francisco remained uninhabited and many of its dependencies passed to the municipal government. The church itself remained in use, maintained by the Third Order of Saint Francis; at the beginning of the 20th century it became a parish church. The complete history of Esperandeu's altarpiece is unknown but the central panel was in the collection of Cesário de Aragón, Marqués de Casas Torres, in Madrid until around 1910 when he sold it to the Lázaro Collection, later the Museo Lázaro Galdeano.[28] In 1952, fragments of some of the narratives were found in the detritus of a pile of wood used for roof repairs stored under the eaves.[29] Now in the *Casa Consistorial* in Tarazona, they represent fragments of three scenes from the *banco* (*The Kiss of Judas, The Washing of Feet* and *The Flagellation*) and two from the Life of the Virgin (*The Circumcision* and *Christ among the Doctors*).[30]

Could our *Crucifixion* have been a part of this *retablo* as well? The measurement of the central panel of Esperandeu's altarpiece is 167 x 107 cm., the *Crucifixion* measures 145 x 100 cm. Normally, the *Crucifixion,* occupying as it does part of the central vertical section of the *retablo,* would be as wide as the main image but sometimes there are discrepancies, particularly if there is an intervening panel with the *Coronation of the Virgin* that could taper at the top (as was the case for the *Retablo of the Virgin* from Tosos, discussed below).

73

he looting of religious artwork triggered by the *desamortazación* of 1835 was neither the first nor the last that Spain endured. Napoleon's soldiers made off with a lot of goods - as they did throughout Europe - during their occupation of Spain between 1808 and 1814 and there were other *desamortazaciones* as well. But Spain itself suffered even greater destruction of religious places and the objects within them during the Spanish Civil War (1936-1939). This was particularly acute at the very beginning, when General Franco's July coup triggered uprisings by leftist coalitions of Anarchists, Anarcho-Syndicalists, Socialists, Marxists and Stalinists as well as disgruntled farmers, underpaid industrial workers, and plain thugs. Churches all over the Iberian Peninsula, seen as unfairly privileged, were burned and looted, as were the ostentatious houses of the aristocracy and wealthy urban bourgeoisie.[31]

Fig. 17. Blasco de Grañén. *Retablo Mayor*, Lanaja.

Two of Grañén's large altarpieces and some smaller pieces were lost. The big *retablos* were dedicated to the Virgin Mary, one in the town of Lanaja (**Fig. 17**), the other in Ontiñena (**Fig. 18**).[32] Both of these towns were under the jurisdiction of the great Monastery and Royal Pantheon at Sigena and both were commissioned, along with some painted tombs, by its Prioress, Beatriz de Cornel (1427-51). The Lanaja altarpiece was documented to the year 1437 and, while no contracts or payments concerning the one at Ontiñena survive, the Prioress's coat of arms appeared on the *guardapolvos* of both.[33] In size and in content, the two altarpieces were very similar. Only two panels from Lanaja survive (they are now in the Museo de Bellas Artes de Zaragoza) and nothing remains from Ontiñena but fortunately the altarpieces had been studied and photographed in detail in 1933 before they were destroyed.[34]

Both altarpieces had, as their central panel, the Esperandeu de Santa Fe and Albalate-style enthroned Virgin.

74

The Ontiñena altarpiece was virtually intact except for its tabernacle and shows how the Albalate and Esperandeu Virgins would have looked originally. In the pre-war photograph only the upper portion of the central image could be seen (**Fig. 18**), as the large, baroque tabernacle which was added cut off the lower half of the panel and presumably also replaced the style of tabernacle found in Anento.[35] Like the Virgin for Albalate, her *embutido* halo was surrounded by a dozen gold stars and like both the other images of the Virgin she held lilies in her right hand and the young Jesus made his usual gesture of blessing (**Fig. 18a**). It is hard to determine how many angels were playing instruments around her.

Above this image was a panel of the *Coronation of the Virgin* with, crowning the central zone, a *Crucifixion* quite similar to the painting published here. There were eighteen panels with scenes from the life of the Virgin, plus six more in the *banco* with the usual passion episodes. The ensemble has a stepped configuration, so that the outer top narratives are shorter than the others; this whole layout is similar to the

Fig. 18. Blasco de Grañén. *Retablo Mayor*, Ontiñena.

big altarpiece at Anento but less complicated in that only the Virgin appears. The framing was luxurious with peaked canopies of *linternas* on top and faceted, slightly projecting *tubas* over the narratives below it. Even the *guardapolvos* were decorated with images of saints as well as the prioress's coat of arms and, completely occupying the apse, was a *sotabanco* under the *banco* with another, narrower, horizontal strip with prophet's heads in roundels. Flanking them were two painted gothic portals, one at either end, to give access to the space behind the structure. They generally had images of Sts. Peter and Paul. The *sotabanco* and doors appeared more often in high altar *retablos* later in the century and this may be one of the earliest. With the addition of the doors, the *retablo* becomes more than just a series of paintings; it merges into the architecture.

Fig. 18a. Blasco de Grañén. *Virgin and Child* from the *Retablo Mayor*, Ontiñena.

The altarpiece from Lanaja entered the 20th century in a more mutilated condition. It was painted for the parish church of Our Lady of the Assumption and a second payment receipt from 1437, the only extant document, was published by Lacarra.[36] The church's two naves and two apses, divided by a large pointed arch nearly spanning both bays of the structure (**Fig. 19**), are unusual for the time and place. The northern, Cistercian nave was apparently built first, in the 13th century, and the second somewhat longer one was added a century later.[37] In 1936, Lanaja was on the Aragonese battle front, conquered from the Falangists and occupied first by the anti-Stalinist but Marxist PUOM, later fiercely bombed and finally recaptured by the Falangists. Grañén's altarpiece was set on fire, as was everything in the building's interior, in the first days of the conflict.[38]

When Post, the first art historian to examine the work *in situ*, wrote about it in 1930, the *retablo* could no longer be seen in its original state. A smaller, sculpted baroque altarpiece had been installed over the painted one. The original central panel and some of the narratives had been moved to the left wall of this nave, the *banco* had been removed with only portions of its upper framing left, and only eight of the large narratives were

76

Fig. 19. Blasco de Grañén. *Our Lady of the Assumption*, Lanaja.

Fig. 20. Blasco de Grañén. *Adoration of the Magi*, Lanaja retable now in Museo de Bellas Artes, Zaragoza.

visible behind the newer installation.[39] Post noted that the fifteen narratives were quite large and showed, as at Ontiñena, scenes from the life of the Virgin and Christ's passion. He thought that the *Coronation of the Virgin,* was almost as big as the central image and, as in Ontiñena, had probably been placed above it. The one panel certainly missing was its *Crucifixion.*[40] The altarpiece and its individual panels were photographed in 1933. The two panels that were known to have been salvaged are now in the *Museo de Bellas Artes* of Zaragoza. They represent two narratives: *The Annunciation to St. Anne,* which is missing its right top portion, and the *Adoration of the Magi* which is intact. Even in their present state both panels are quite large (The *St. Anne* measures 156 x 107 cm., the *Adoration,* 151 x 108 cm).[41]

These compositions are similar in style and content to others produced by the workshop.[42] An idea of this thematic closeness and variation can be seen by comparing the *Adoration of the Magi* from Lanaja (**Fig. 20**) with a panel from Anento (**Fig. 21**). The two compositions are reversed, which may have something to do with their original placement in relation to the large image. Both have stage-set stables with thatched roofs with

Fig. 21. Blasco de Grañén. *Adoration of the Magi*, Anento.

Fig. 22. Blasco de Grañén. *Virgin* from the *Retablo Mayor*, Lanaja.

quaint openings. The costumes of the kings at Anento are richer, with crowns, while those at Lanaja wear hats. At Lanaja Joseph, with a polygonal halo, is outside the little fence; at Anento he is in the stable. The ox and ass appear at Lanaja, but there are two shepherds at Anento. However both panels are unmistakably from the same workshop and have a similar range of colours, cast of characters and lack of depth and clarity of gesture.

78

The central panel (**Fig.22**), in rather poor condition when it was photographed with much paint loss along the joins of its support, is the fourth of Grañén's *Virgin and Child with Musical Angels* to follow the above template. This one has eight musical angels and, although the Virgin's halo lacks the dozen gold stars of the Lady of the Apocalypse, her feet rest on the crescent moon from the same source. Here she reaches towards a pot of flowers while Jesus holds a pomegranate branch. Again, though all of these Virgin panels come from the same basic cartoon, the painter varies each one in subtle ways, as is also the case where there are repeated narrative compositions.

A harrowing attempt to prevent the destruction of these altarpieces was related in the eyewitness account of the Catalan sculptor Apel.les Fenosa, who was serving with a militia company in Aragon and rescued what he could:

> 'It's thankless work, and the people don't understand it. One day they wanted to kill me, confusing me with a robber who wanted to profit by looting.
> Ungrateful because of not understanding. Ungrateful because of those of bad
> faith and ignorance and for those who know what this is all worth without having done anything to save it; when they see it saved, they accuse you of being a robber and a vampire in the town…'
> '….At Grañén, we arrived when they were taking apart a magnificent, splendid retablo to make firewood. We collected it piece by piece, to the last splinter. But the most beautiful, the most valuable was already lost.'
> '….At La Naja [sic], the wind has already carried away the cinders of a very important treasure, known all over the world. We have only saved two very good [panels from] *retablos* from the early 15th century.
> I know that history will thank me for the agonies and the bad times through which I passed to save them.'[43]

The Aragonese press and some scholars have suggested that our *Crucifixion* might have been another panel saved from Lanaja and not reported.[44] The dimensions of the two surviving narratives - very large for side panels, with widths of 107 and 108 cm. - would imply that the centre strip was wider still. Since the *Crucifixion's* width measures 100 cm., it seems unlikely that it came from this *retablo*, unless the Lanaja *retablo* by Grañén's workshop followed a different model, like the one painted for the Parish Church of Tosos, again dedicated to the Virgin Mary, with a different image for the central panel which was surmounted by

Fig. 23. Blasco de Grañén. *Coronation of the Virgin* and *Crucifixion*, Tosos.

a *Coronation of the Virgin* and a much smaller *Crucifixion* above that (**fig. 23**).[45] The original configuration of the whole *retablo* had long been dismantled and, as at Lajana, the panels were recycled into the later Baroque altarpiece. In 2011 it was restored and reassembled by La Escuela Taller Juan Arnaldín, de la Diputación Provincial de Zaragoza (DPZ), who have skillfully invoked the 15th century typology of the altarpiece. The ratio of the *Crucifixion's* width here seems to match the narratives but the altarpiece from Tosos is taller and narrower than those of Ontiñena and Lanaja. In addition, the Tosos *Crucifixion* has a gabled, curving frame (called a *chambrana* in 15th century contracts) flanked by pinnacles. Our *Cruxifixion* has a flat top with a simple arch within the panel at the top; it would most likely have been topped by a *linterna* like the one at Ontiñena.

There is, however, one more *retablo* dedicated to the Virgin that could provide a viable candidate for our *Crucifixion*. This is an altarpiece that was in the collection of the family of Barcelona industrialist and financier, Robert Robert i Surís (1851-1929), usually referred to as the Marqués de Robert.[46] He is best remembered for the sumptuous mansion he built on the Passeig de Gràcia, the most fashionable street in Barcelona. It was eventually put up for sale in 1934 by his successors, who relocated their baronial seat elsewhere, and it underwent several conversions. On the eve of the Civil War the building became the seat of the *Generalitat's* Department of Culture. The Robert family took it back in 1944, converting it to a hotel and casino. There followed years of litigation and after many vicissitudes the post-Franco *Generalitat* acquired, restored and modified it and it is now known once again as the Palau Robert and is an information centre for Catalonia.

The original Marqués collected art although it seems never to have been catalogued but Gudiol mentions '*retablos* of the Marqués de Robert' being saved around August 1936, so they must have been rescued from the Robert residence during the wholesale looting and destruction that went on in Barcelona during the initial days of the uprising in July 1936. In this trove was apparently a *retablo* dedicated to the Virgin by the Grañén workshop as Lacarra cites a panel of the Virgin and Child that went to the Ibercaja Collection and which is now in the Museo Camón Aznar in Zaragoza that was known to have been in the Robert collection in 1937. At least twelve panels, all showing scenes from the life of the Virgin were in the same collection.[47] Five of them, *Joaquin and Anne Expelled from the Temple* (116 x 68 cm.), *The Birth of the Virgin* (116 x 71 cm.), *The Pentecost* (113 x 68 cm.), *The Death of the Virgin* (120 x 70.5 cm.) and *the Virgin Appearing to St. Thomas* (112.5 x 67 cm.) went into the collection of Mariano Espinal in Barcelona and he later gave them to the Museo de Bellas Artes in Bilbao in 1959.[48] In 1999, the Bilbao Museum was able to purchase the *Presentation in the Temple* as well.[49] The present location of the remaining six panels, whose subject matter was *The Meeting at the Golden Gate, The Adoration of the Magi, the Circumcision, the Annunciation of the Virgin's Death, the Funeral Procession of the Virgin* and the *Burial of the Virgin* is unknown.

Since the Marqués de Robert owned these panels until at least 1937 and, so far as is known, none were framed, nobody knows their provenance but their removal from their church or convent probably took place much earlier, perhaps in the aftermath of 1835. The Marqués evidently remained silent about how and where he acquired them.

The central *Virgin and Child* panel now in Zaragoza (**Fig. 24**) is quite large (214 x 109 cm.) and the number of panels again suggests a *retablo mayor* although the Bilbao and Zaragoza components are smaller than those in

Fig. 24. Blasco de Grañén – *Virgin and Child*, Zaragoza,

Fig. 25. Blasco de Grañén. *Birth of the Virgin* from the Marqués de Robert Retable, Museo de Bellas Artes, Bilbao.

Ontiñena and Lanaja. It also appears that both *Crucifixion* and *banco* were detached and sold off separately.

The *Virgin and Child* has Blasco's typical iconography: six angels, four with musical instruments, no apocalyptic references or lilies, the Virgin holding the Christ Child, the Child holding a bird but the composition is taller and narrower and the elaborate scalloped border at the base of the throne is far more pronounced - is this perhaps a later template? The extant narratives are similar to other workshop productions with, as usual, variations (for example, a maidservant offers St. Anne a roast chicken in the *Birth of the Virgin)* (**Fig. 25**). It is unfortunate that no contract seems to exist for this altarpiece, since the choice of narratives is somewhat unusual: six refer to the Virgin's young life, and six to the end of her life and her death. The scenes of the Virgin's burial and of her giving her belt to St. Thomas are extremely rare. The burial scene, however, also found at Ontiñena, though here, instead of the St. Thomas episode, there is an equally rare scene of the Virgin on her deathbed giving a palm to John the Evangelist. Is it possible that the Robert Collection retablo was also commissioned by Beatriz Cornel, and that these rarities reflect her personal choice? [50]

iven the unknown provenance of our *Crucifixion* it might originally have been part of the *retablo,* though it is listed nowhere, but then the *banco* was not inventoried either. Again, its measurements are narrower than those of the central panel in Zaragoza, so no conclusions may be drawn.

Of course, the *Crucifixion* may come from a *retablo* not dedicated to the Virgin. Lacarra discusses and reproduces documentation for altarpieces dedicated to Sts. Martin of Tours, Lucy, Fabian and Sebastian, James, Nicholas, Zita of Lucca, Michael and Thomas, but many of them have not survived. Museums and collections also have isolated panels by the Grañén workshop and, according to Post, several of these turned up in the hands of dealers in the 1930s and 1940s.[51]

With an enterprise as extensive as Blasco de Grañén's in Zaragoza it is hard to narrow down a composition as ubiquitous as a *Crucifixion* (many are not even listed in contracts since they are an expected component) to a specific altarpiece and there is always the possibility that it is the sole survivor of a vanished and unknown *retablo.* The ideal would be to find a detached central image from one of Blasco's *retablos* that measures 100 cm. in width although the possibility of a mystery always remains!

JUDITH SOBRE

1   Nuria Ortiz Valero, 'Calvario,' p. 1, identifies the lady holding up the Virgin as Mary Magdalen, quite feasible as she has long fair hair—a usual attribute. Ortiz Valero, in her essay, offers an excellent analysis of the iconography of many of Blasco de Grañén's works.

2   If the *retablo* were very large a third panel might be inserted between the main effigy and the *Crucifixion*. In altarpieces dedicated to the Virgin this was most often the scene of her coronation.

3   For detailed studies of *retablos* and their function, see Judith Berg Sobré, *Behind the Altar Table, the Development of the Spanish Painted Retablo, 1350-1500,* especially the introduction, pp. 3-11 and chapter 4, pp. 49-71, Columbia, Missouri, the University of Missouri Press, 1989, and also Justin E.A. Kroesen, *Staging the Liturgy, The Medieval Altarpiece in the Iberian Peninsula,* Leuven & Paris, Walpole, Peeters, 2009.

4   The *doyenne* of Blasco studies is Maria del Carmen Lacarra Ducay, who has published numerous articles on the painter, and the definitive monograph, *Blasco de Grañén, Pintor de Retablos (1422-1459),* Zaragoza, Institución Fernando el Católico (C.S.I.C), 2004. This book summarizes all the previous articles, sometimes virtually verbatim, beginning in 1985.

5   Lacarra, (2004), includes a section with transcriptions of all documentation pertaining to the painter and his shop. In this section, she was assisted by Rafael Conde and Delgado de Molina. Ortiz, p. 11 discusses one of the sarcophagi in her article.

6   Chandler R. Post, *A History of Spanish Painting*, 14 Vols., Cambridge, Mass., 1930-1966. Josep Gudiol Ricart, *Pintura Mediæval en Aragón,* Zaragoza, Institución Fernando el Católico, 1971, 75-77, catalogued 26 works attributed to the painter and his circle, still as 'Master of Lanaja'

7   Ana Galilea Antón, *La pintura gótica española en el Museo de Bellas Artes de Bilbao, Bilbao, Bilboko arte ederretako Museoa, S.A., 1995, p. 129.*

8   This practice closely echoes the current day *modus operandi* of contemporary workshops from Kiefer to Murakami.

9   The contract for the Altarpiece of Esprandeu de Santa Fe of 1438, for example, specifically states that the workshop had to cover expenses for transportation and installation. Lacarra (2004), p. 37.

10 Since the advent of the paved road, Anento's wall paintings and restored *retablo* have become a major tourist attraction. See the town's website, http://www.anento.es/. The *retablo*, as well as the wall paintings and other altarpieces of the church, were restored by the Diputación of Zaragoza between 1999 and 2003.

11 A full inventory of the altarpiece's content can be found in Lacarra, 2004, pp. 119-149.

12 Lacarra, pp. 149-152.

13 According to Anento's website, http://www.anento.es/historia.php, its late 15th century population was of 42 households. Its historical claim to fame seems to have been as a place of refuge during the War of the Two Pedros in the 14th century. It had a small castle.

14 For a detailed study of one aspect of Dalmau de Mur's career as a patron, see Katherine Dimitroff, doctoral dissertation, *Unraveling Christ's Passion: Archbishop Dalmau de Mur, Patron and Collector, and Franco-Flemish Tapestries in Fifteenth-Century Spain,* University of Pittsburgh, (2008), accessible at www. http://d-scholarship.pitt.edu/7598/.

15 Post, IV, pp. 624-626, who made the hike to the town in the early 1930s, was only impressed by the altarpiece's size. He described the painting as 'a nondescript, rather countrified international work of c.1430.'

16 A detailed diagram of the *retablo* with mouse-over images for each panel can be found at http://www.anento.es/retablo.php.

17 Lacarra, 2004, p. 154.

18 Lacarra, 2004, p. 48. For some idea of the contemporary worth of the *sueldo* in the Crown of Aragon at this time, see Matilde Miquel Juan, *Retablos, prestigio y dinero*, Universitat de Valencia, Servei de Publicacions, 2008, 258-60. A master stone-cutter at this period received a daily wage of 5 *sueldos*.

19 See Ortiz, pp.4-5 for some variations on the *Crucifixion* from the workshop.

Detail from Fig. 13

20 Lacarra, 2004, 25, quotes a visitor, Vicente Bardaviú Ponz, who wrote a description of it in 1914, noting that it had already been in San José for at least a century. It entered the Museo de Bellas Artes in Zaragoza in 1921.

21 María Teresa Ainaga Andrés and Jesús Criado Mainar, 'El convento de San Francisco de Tarazona (Zaragoza), construcción y reforma de sus edificios medievales,' *Aragón en la Edad Media, XIV-XV, Homenaje a la profesora Carmen Orcástigui Gros,* Universidad de Zaragoza, Facultad de Filosofía y Letras, Zaragoza, 1999, pp. 49-72, p. 62.

22 The actual contract was signed by his son, Loys (or Luís de Santa Fe).

23 Rodrigo Amador de los Ríos, 'El Libro Verde de Aragón,' *Revista de España,* Vol. CVI, September/October 1885, p. 255.

24 These debates were basically with Anti-Pope Benedict XIII, King Ferdinand I of Aragon and Vicent Ferrer, backing the convert Rabbi Jerónimo de Santa Fe (formerly Joshua Ha-Lorki) against some heavily-censored rabbis. See Miguel Angel Motís Dolader , 'En recuerdo de los judíos de Tarazona,' (May 10, 2010) at the Tarbut Sefarad Website, http://www.tarbutsefarad.com/es/juderia-tarazona/3528-en-recuerdo-de-los-judios-de-tarazona.html. For a summary of the debates themselves, see the article on 'Disputations' in *The Jewish Encyclopedia,* http://jewishencyclopedia.com/articles/5226-disputations.

25 Lacarra, 2004 p. 37 reproduces the contract.

26 This was not a new practice, *deasmortizaciónes* began with Carlos IV's prime minister Manual Godoy, and there would be several more. See 'La desamortización,' http://www.laiglesiamayorsectadelahistoria.com/?s=100&a=173.

27 Oscar E. Vázquez, *Inventing the Art Collection; Patrons, Markets and the State in nineteenth-century Spain*, Pennsylvania State University Press, 2001, gives a comprehensive picture of the *desamortizacións* and their consequences for collecting.

28 Carlos Saguar Quer, Fondos Aragoneses del Museo Lázaro Galdeano, *Artigrama* no. 20, 2005, p119 and note 28. According to Saguar, the Marqués de Casa Torres must have owned it for several decades, because he lent it to the *Exposición Histórico-Europea 1892-1893* in Madrid.

29 Lacarra, 2004, p.39, n.35.

30 Lacarra (2004) 41-2, concurring with the earlier opinions of Post and Leandro de Saralegui, suggested that a panel of the *Presentation in the Temple*, which had also been in the Casa Torres collection, was also part of the altarpiece, but its *embutido* haloes are very different from the restored fragments with flat haloes in Tarazona.

31 See the eye-witness account by Josep Gudiol Ricart on pages 17-42.

32 A smaller triptych with a carved center, made for the brothers Pascual and Pedro Bernat in 1439 for the parish church of Belchite, was destroyed during the battle and bombardment of that town in 1937. See Lacarra (2004) pp.171-3).

33 Lacarra (2004) pp. 28-36, and 158-170 (she also discusses the surviving painted tombs by Grañén's workshop.

34 Post, III, pp. 333-334, discussed the *retablo* from Lanaja, and subsequently (IV, 638-9) that of Ontiñena. But the most detailed study of both altarpieces was done in 1936 by José and Joaquín Albareda, who discussed those from Lanaja in 'Los Primitivos de la Iglesia de Lanaja' in a two-part article in *Aragon*, February, 1936, pp. 34-36, and March, 1936, pp. 54-56. Two months later, they published 'El Retablo Mayor de la Parroquial de Ontiñena,' *Aragon,* May, 1936, pp 93-96. By July of the same year, both had perished.

35 Albarado Brothers, 'El Retablo Mayor de la Parroquia de Ontiñena', p. 95.

36 Lacarra (2004), p. 28.

37 See 'Iglesia Parroquial de la Asunción', http://lanaja.com/iglesias_la_asuncion.php. When the Albarado Brothers visited it in 1936, they remarked on its unusual plan and noted that its structure was in rather poor condition.

38 See the memoirs of Gudiol Ricard for two eyewitness accounts of the burning of the church and the rescue of two of the *retablo's* panels.

39 The two outer *Linternas* of the top zone survived.

40 Post, III, pp.333-334. Post mentions one panel that he could not identify, hidden behind the later altarpiece.

41 Lacarra (2004, p. 28 n. 19) states that one other panel showing the *Birth of the Virgin*, survived the fire in terrible condition; according to a photograph of it in the Institut Amatller d'Art Històric, it was in the collection of the Museu Nacional d'Art de Catalunya in Barcelona but is not now listed among its holdings.

42 Lacarra, 1990, pp. 22-26. Both have been beautifully restored.

43 Fenosa is quoted in the article 'Catalunya ha salvat a Aragó un trésor artistic,' *Mirador. Setmanari de Literatura, Art i Politica*, Any VIII Núm 397, Barcelona, dijous, 3 desembre 1936 (segona epoca), pp.8-7. The English translation is mine. The 16ᵗʰ century *Retablo Mayor* of Grañén was salvaged and is back in its church.

44 P. Ciria, 'La DGA déjà escapar también la compra de una pieza del retablo de Lanaja subastada en París, *El Heraldo* (Zaragoza), April 4, 2009. 'We know that it was by Blasco de Grañén but we cannot be certain that it came from Lanaja. Detailed studies would be necessary to determine this.' (my translation)

45 Lacarra (2004), pp.190-194. See also Tosos' municipal website, http://tosos.webcindario.com/tosos/paginas/retabloiglesia.html. Before 2011, the *Coronation* and *Crucifixion* were in a side chapel, separated from the panels in the high altar.

46 http://www20.gencat.cat/portal/site/PalauRobert?newLang=ca_ES The title was bestowed upon him by Pope Leo XIII around 1890 and he was later given additional aristocratic titles in 1891 and finally in 1907 Alfonxo XIII made him a 'Grandee of Spain' and Count of Toroella y Montgrí.

47 Lacarra (2004, 195) does not give her source for this information but she listed eleven narratives panels as *Expulsion of Anne and Joachim from the Temple, The Meeting at the Golden Gate, Birth of the Virgin, Presentation of Mary in the Temple, Circumcision, Epiphany, Pentecost, Annunciation of the Virgin's Death, Death of the Virgin, Burial of the Virgin,* and *The Virgin appearing to St. Thomas*. This same list plus the *Funeral Procession of the Virgin*, is listed among the photographic holdings in the Frick Art Reference Library in New York. All were purchased from the Arxiu d'Arqueologia Catalana (Barcelona) on June 1, 1936.

48 Galilea Antón, pp.132-135.

49 Galilea Antón was given photographs of two of them by the Espinal family, who didn't did not know what happened to them, The *Presentation in the Temple was one of these*.

50 On the other hand, they are not found at Lanaja.

51 See, for example, Chandler R. Post, *A History of Spanish Painting,* vol. VII (1938) 802-816, and vol. VIII (1941), pp. 67

EXHIBITION CATALOGUES
THE MATTHIESEN GALLERY, LONDON 1978
Those marked ¶ Matthiesen Gallery in association with Stair Sainty Matthiesen
Those marked ‡ edited and published with Stair Sainty Matthiesen

1979   *British Printmakers 1812–1840*.
        52 pages with 431 items, many illustrated (edited by James Ingram – out of print).

1980   *Symbolist and Art Nouveau Prints – Autumn Catalogue*.
        80 pages fully illustrated (edited by James Ingram – out of print).

1981   *Important Italian Baroque Paintings, 1600–1700*.
        An exhibition in aid of *The Frescoes by Guarino at Solofra* damaged by earthquake.
        Foreword by Alvar González-Palacios.
        100 pages, 22 colour plates, 34 black and white illustrations. £20 or $30 inc.
        p. & p. (scarce).

1981   *Fine Prints and Drawings: England, America and Europe*.
        60 pages with 173 items, many illustrated (edited by James Ingram – out of print).

1983   *Early Italian Paintings and Works of Art, 1300–1480*.
        An exhibition in aid of The Friends of the *Fitzwilliam Museum*.
        Introductory essay by Dr Dillian Gordon on 'Painting Techniques in Italy, 1270–1450'.
        127 pages, 22 colour plates, 34 black and white illustrations.
        £12 or $18 inc. p. & p.

1984   *From Borso to Cesare d'Este, 1450–1628: The School of Ferrara*.
        An exhibition in aid of *The Courtauld Institute Trust Appeal Fund*.
        Ten introductory essays on Ferrara and aspects of Ferrarese art by Cecil Gould,
        Lanfranco Caretti, Claudio Gallico, Vincenzo Fontana, Thomas Tuohy,
        Emmanuele Mattaliano, Giorgio Bassani, Giuliano Briganti, Alastair Smith,
        with charts and Concordat of Ferrarese paintings in British public collections.
        200 pages, 50 colour plates, 84 black and white illustrations. £15 or $23 inc. p. & p.

¶ 1984   *The Macchiaioli*.
        122 pages, fully illustrated (out of print).

¶ 1984 *Three Friends of the Impressionists: Boldini, De Nittis, Zandomeneghi*.
53 pages, fully illustrated (out of print).

1985 *Around 1610: The Onset of the Baroque*.
An exhibition on behalf of Famine Relief in Ethiopia by *The Relief Society of Tigray*.
Introduction by Sir Ellis Waterhouse.
120 pages, 33 colour plates, 22 black and white illustrations (scarce). £12 or $18 inc. p. & p.

‡ 1985 *The First Painters of the King: French Royal Taste from Louis XIV to the Revolution*.
Catalogue by Colin Bailey, including three comprehensive essays by Philip Conisbee,
Jean-Luc Bordeaux and Thomas Gaehtgens. Introduction by Guy Stair Sainty.
Inventory of paintings by the 'First Painters in Public Collections in the USA'.
144 pages, 21 colour plates, 243 black and white illustrations (out of print).

1986 *Baroque III: 1620–1700*.
An exhibition in memory of Sir Ellis Waterhouse and on behalf of *The National
Art Collections Fund*.
Introduction by Sir Peter Wakefield. Essays by Francis Haskell, Cecil Gould,
Francis Russell, Charles McCorquodale and Craig Felton.
152 pages, 15 colour plates, 30 black and white illustrations. £15 or $23 inc. p. & p.

‡ 1986 *An Aspect of Collecting Taste*.
Introduction by Guy Stair Sainty.
68 pages, 24 colour plates, 7 black and white illustrations (out of print).

1987 *Paintings from Emilia, 1500–1700*.
An exhibition held in New York at the Newhouse Galleries Inc.
Foreword by Professor Sydney J. Freedberg. Introduction by Emmanuele Mattaliano.
150 pages, 33 colour plates, 63 black and white illustrations.
£15 or $23 inc. p. & p.

1987 *The Settecento: Italian Rococo and Early Neoclassical Paintings, 1700–1800*.
An exhibition held on behalf of *Aids Crisis Trust (UK)* and *The American Foundation
for Aids Research (USA)*.
Introduction by Charles McCorquordale. Essays by Francis Russell, Edgar Peters
and Catherine Whistler.
200 pages, 31 colour plates, 88 black and white illustrations.
£15 or $23 inc. p. & p.

‡   1987   *François Boucher and his Circle and Influence*.
          Introduction by Regina Shoolman Slatkin.
          136 pages, 18 colour plates, 80 black and white illustrations (out of print).

    1989   *A Selection of French Paintings 1700–1840 Offered for Sale*.
          An exhibition on behalf of Médecins Sans Frontières.
          154 pages, 42 colour plates, 77 black and white illustrations. £10 or $15 inc. p. & p.

¶   1991   *Louis-Léopold Boilly's 'L'Entreé du Jardin Turc'*.
          'Spectacle and Display in Boilly's "L'Entreé du Jardin Turc"'. Essay by Susan
          L. Siegfried. 36 pages, 25 plates. £10 or $15 inc. p. & p.

¶   1991   *Eighty Years of French Painting from Louis XVI to the Second Republic 1775–1855*.
          70 pages, 20 colour plates. £12 or $17 inc. p. & p.

    1991   *Pre-Raphaelite Sculpture. Nature and Imagination in British Sculpture 1 1848–1914*.
          An exhibition organized by Joanna Barnes in association with The Henry Moore
          Foundation. Hardback book to accompany the exhibition with 174 pages fully illustrated.

¶   1993   *Fifty Paintings 1535–1825*.
          To celebrate ten years of collaboration between The Matthiesen Gallery, London,
          and Stair Sainty Matthiesen, New York.
          216 pages, 50 colour plates, numerous black and white text illustrations.
          £20 or $32 inc. p. & p.

¶   1996   *Paintings 1600–1912*.
          144 pages, 26 colour plates. £12 or $20 inc. p. & p.

¶   1996   *Romance and Chivalry: History and Literature reflected
          in Early Nineteenth Century French Painting*.
          Introduction (40 pages) by Guy Stair Sainty, twelve essays, catalogue,
          appendix of salons 801–1824 and bibliography.
          Hardback book, 300 pages, fully illustrated with 90 colour plates and 100 black
          and white illustrations. £50 or $80 inc. p. & p. (scarce).

    1996   *Gold Backs 1250–1480*.
          An exhibition held on behalf of The Arthritis and Rheumatism Council.
          Foreword and four essays. Limited edition hardback catalogue of the exhibition
          held in London and New York.
          154 pages, fully illustrated with 37 colour plates and 54 black
          and white text illustrations. £40 or $65 inc. p. & p. (scarce).

1997 *An Eye on Nature: Spanish Still Life Painting from Sanchez Cotan to Goya*.
Foreword by Patrick Matthiesen. Catalogue entries by Dr William B. Jordan.
Hard and softback catalogue of the exhibition held in New York.
153 pages, fully illustrated with 23 colour plates and 65 black and white text
illustrations. £30 or $50 inc. p. & p. (scarce).

1999 *Collectanea 1700–1800*.
Hardback catalogue of the exhibition held in London and New York.
220 pages, fully illustrated with 46 colour plates. £30 or $50 inc. p. & p.

¶ 1999 *An Eye on Nature II: The Gallic Prospect*.
French Landscape Painting 1785–1900.
Foreword by Patrick Matthiesen and Guy Stair Sainty. Hardback catalogue of the
exhibition held in New York.
195 pages, fully illustrated with 37 full colour plates and 65 black and white illustrations
(many full page). £35 or $50 inc. p. & p.

2000 *Marzio Tamer: Recent Paintings*.
Exhibition held on behalf of *The World Wildlife Fund*.
Softback catalogue, 64 pages, 61 illustrations. £10 or $15 inc. p. & p.

¶ 2001 *European Paintings – From 1600–1917*.
Baroque, Rococo, Romanticism, Realism, Futurism.
Spring softback catalogue, 110 pages, 29 colour plates, 26 black and white illustrations.
£15 or $25 inc. p. & p.

2001 *2001: An Art Odyssey 1500–1720*.
Preface by Errico di Lorenzo and Patrick Matthiesen. 'El Bosque de Los Nino'
by Patrick Matthiesen. Foreword, reminiscences and detailed inventory records
of the Costa seventeenth-century archives by Patrick Matthiesen.
Hardbound millennium catalogue with special binding, 360 pages, 58 colour plates,
184 black and white illustrations. £35 or $60 plus p. & p.

2002 *Andrea Del Sarto Rediscovered*.
Essay by Beverly Louise Brown.
Hardback catalogue, 60 pages, 9 colour plates, 18 black and white illustrations.
Limited edition. £15 or $25 inc. p. & p.

2002 *Gaspar Van Wittel and Il Porto di Ripetta.*
Essay by Laura Laureati.
Hardback catalogue, 52 pages, 2 colour plates, 23 black and white illustrations.
Limited edition. £15 or $25 inc. p. & p.

2003 *Chardin's 'Têtes d' Études au Pastel'.*
Essay by Philip Conisbee.
Hardback catalogue, 33 pages, 2 colour plates, 12 black and white illustrations.
Limited edition. £15 or $25 inc. p. & p.

2004 *Bertin's Ideal Landscapes.*
Essay by Chiara Stefani.
Hardback catalogue, 46 pages, 2 colour plates, 27 black and white illustrations.
Limited edition. £15 or $25 inc. p. & p.

2004 *Polidoro da Caravaggio: Polidoro and La Lignamine's Messina Lamentation.*
Text by P. L. Leone De Castris.
Hardback catalogue, 62 pages, 11 colour plates, 15 black and white illustrations.
Limited edition. £15 or $25 inc. p. & p.

2004 *Virtuous Virgins, Classical Heroines, Romantic Passion and the Art of Suicide.*
Text by Beverly L. Brown.
Hardback catalogue, 60 pages, 2 colour plates, 21 black and white illustrations.
Limited edition. £15 or $25 inc. p. & p.

2007 *Manet, Berthe Morisot.*
Text by Charles Stuckey
Hardback catalogue, 32 pages, 11 colour plates. Limited edition.
£15 or $25 inc. p. & p.

2007 *Jacobello Del Fiore: His Oeuvre and a Sumptuous Crucifixion.*
Text by Daniele Benati.
Hardback catalogue, 80 pages, 12 colour plates, 15 black and white illustrations.
Limited edition. £15 or $25 inc. p. & p.

2008 *Jacques Blanchard: Myth and Allegory.*
Texts by Christopher Wright and Andrea Gates.
Hardback catalogue, 5 colour plates, 6 black and white illustrations. Limited edition.
£15 or $25 inc. p. & p.

2009   *A Florentine Four Seasons*.
Text by Andrea Gates.
Hardback catalogue, 96 pages, 11 colour plates, 21 black and white illustrations.
Limited edition. £15or $25 inc. p. & p.

2009   *Théodore Rousseau. A Magnificent Obsession: La Ferme dans les Landes*.
Texts by Simon Kelly and Andrea Gates.
Softback catalogue, 52 pages, 3 colour plates, 16 black and white illustrations.
Limited edition. £15or $25 inc. p. & p.

2009   *The Mystery of Faith: An Eye on Spanish Sculpture 1550 - 1750*.
Various texts.
Hardback silk blocked and bound. 300 pages.112 colour plates, 153 black and white illustrations.
£90 or Euros 100 plus post and packing (charge varies according to destination).

2010   *Révolution • République • Empire • Restauration*.
Hardback catalogue, 84 pages, 11 colour plates, 39 black and white illustrations.
£15 or $25 inc. p. & p.

2011   *James Ward: A Lioness with a Heron*.
Text by Andrea Gates.
Hardback catalogue, 48 pages, 3 colour plates, 14 black and white illustrations.
£15 or $25 inc. p. & p.

2012   *Liberation & Deliverance - Luca Giordano's Liberation of St. Peter*.
Texts by Helen Langdon and Giuseppe Scavizzi.
Hardback catalogue, 60 pages, 7 colour plates, 21 colour and black and white illustrations. £15 or $25 inc. p. & p.

2012   *Joseph Wright of Derby:Virgil's Tomb & The Grand Tour*
Texts by Jenny Uglow and Bart Thurber.
Hardback catalogue, 76 pages, 5 colour plates and 74 black and white illustrations.
£15 or $25 inc. p. & p.

2013   *A Winning End-game: Francis Cotes,William Earle Welby and His Wife Penelope*
Text by Jenny Uglow.
Hardback catalogue, 48 pages, 6 colour plates and 17 black and white illustrations.
£15 or $25 inc. p. & p.

2013   *Vision & Ecstasy: Giovanni Benedetto Castiglione's St. Francis.*
        Texts by Helen Langdon and Jonathan Bober.
        Hardback catalogue, 84 pages, 20 colour plates and 47 black and white illustrations.
        £15 or $25 inc. p. & p.

2014   *Fatal Attraction: Sex and Avarice in Dosso Dossi's Jupiter and Semele*
        Text by Beverly Brown.
        Hardback catalogue, 84 pages, 46 colour plates and 26 black and white illustrations.
        £18 or $30 inc. p. & p.

2015   *Juan de Sevilla*
        Text by Judith Sobre
        82 pages, 24 colour plates and 4 black and white illustrations.
        £18 or $30 inc. p. & p..

MATTHIESEN

EXPERTS, AGENTS, APPRAISERS AND DEALERS IN
EUROPEAN PAINTINGS
FROM THE FOURTEENTH TO THE NINETEENTH CENTURIES

This catalogue was issued as a limited edition of 650 copies. It was printed in Turin and bound in Milan, Italy, using Garda Gloss 200 gsm soft fine art paper and Komori Lithone S 29 presses in five colours. Illustrations were printed in dry proof quadratone.

The typeface used in the body of the text is based on the Gill Family using his Perpetua font designed by Eric Gill between 1925 and 1929 for Stanley Morrison, the typographical advisor to Monotype.
Titles are set in English Gothic 17th and subtitles are set in Mayflower Antique fonts. Ornaments are Micro Fleurons font while the capitals are Gothic illuminate font.

Title page and half title set in English Gothic 17th.
The cover is blocked in English Gothic 17th while the spine is set in Mayflower Antique font.

Photographic credits: Comparatives courtesy of The Fundación Lázaro Galdiano, Madrid; The Prado Museum, Madrid; The Toledo Museum of Art; Marcos Nieto; Prudence Cuming Associates, London.

The catalogue text was written by JUDITH SOBRE.

Graphic layout and editing by PATRICK MATTHIESEN.

Colour origination by *Fotomec Srl.* and production by *Tipo Stampa.*

This catalogue was designed by PATRICK MATTHIESEN.
The texts are © MATTHIESEN LTD and JUDITH SOBRE.
Copyright Reserved March MMXV by MATTHIESEN LTD., LONDON.

ISBN 978-0-9575459-3-9